CONSTELLATIONS

12 PIECED ASTROLOGICAL BLOCKS, 8 PERSONALIZED SEWING PROJECTS

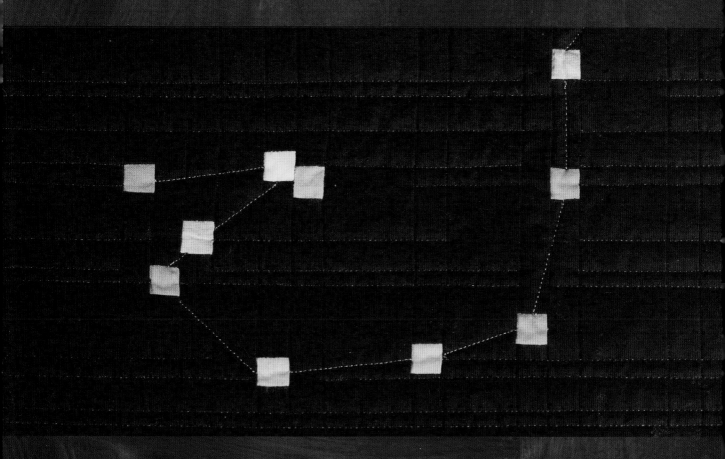

Amber Platzer Corcoran and Jaime Jennings

Published in 2017 by Lucky Spool Media, LLC
www.luckyspool.com
info@luckyspool.com

Text © Amber Platzer Corcoran and Jaime Jennings
Editor: Susanne Woods
Designer: Page + Pixel
Illustrator: Courtney Kyle
Photographs by: Holly DeGroot
(except where noted)
Photographs on pages 8-33 by Amber Platzer Corcoran

9 8 7 6 5 4 3 2 1
First Edition
Printed in China

Library of Congress Cataloging-in-Publication Data
available upon request

IBSN: 978-1940655277

Acknowledgements
We are thankful to our shop's
community of folks who are always
so enthusiastic about what we do!
We couldn't have created this book
without some amazing folks—
big thanks to Susanne Woods,
Jason Beck, Susan Santistevan,
Caitlin Vannoy, Kaylee Lockhart,
Shawna Doering, Grace Snow and
Keely Shaw. Thank you all to the
stars and back!

TABLE OF CONTENTS

INTRODUCTION

Meaningful Modern Style

There is nothing quite so universally beautiful as the stars suspended in the night sky. The constellations above have captured our imagination throughout history. They are the oldest storybook in the world. No matter where you find yourself, you can glance up at the stars and share the stories that are written there. Something is magical about these seemingly random sprinklings of stars that we know as constellations, recognizable by any human who has ever looked up with curiosity to the night sky.

I was inspired to make my first patchwork Constellation Block, Taurus, as a throw pillow for my own home. As someone whose style is a balancing act between minimalism and textile devotee, I was interested in something handmade yet minimal enough to work with my mishmash of other beloved home accessories. I had an idea for making something mostly solid, focusing on negative space with just a few peeks of a contrasting patchwork. Sketching, I started to think of stars, and I decided to patchwork a constellation of my astrological sign.

I thoroughly enjoyed the process of mapping out the stars for my block. When folks asked for a pattern for their own star sign, I was happy to oblige. Much of what inspires my designs is the community of passionately supportive and inspiring makers who come together at Fancy Tiger Crafts, the bustling Denver shop I share with my business partner, Jaime Jennings. Once I had mapped out all the constellations in patchwork, the twelve blocks were published through our shop as small pattern cards. It was always my dream to collect these constellation patterns together into a book and to include a variety of projects to make from them.

Jaime and I have together developed eight magical sewing and quilting projects for these modern constellation blocks. To bring the blocks to life, you may want to join the stars with embroidery or quilting. These lines will illuminate the shapes of the astrological symbols that we imagine in the night sky. Diagrams are shown on page 74, toward the end of the book.

  –Amber

"No matter where we are, we'll always share the same sky. We can always find each other in the same constellation."
— Roshani Chokshi

PART 1

THE BLOCKS

These 20″ blocks bring the sparse beauty of the celestial into your home with minimalist patchwork. The stars in each block are placed precisely with satisfyingly methodical step-by-step construction, mimicking the organic beauty of our night sky. Each block is made up of simple strip piecing, stars peppered in deliberately to create the constellation. Choose a dark indigo or black for your background fabric and one or more colors of scraps for your stars. You can even fussy cut stars for your patchwork (see the Astrological Tea Towel project, page 58). The blocks can be used in a myriad of projects. In the second part of this book there are plenty of project ideas to create with a single or several blocks.

MATERIALS + TOOLS + TIPS

Materials

For each 20″ Constellation Block, you will need:

- ⅝ yard background fabric
- Scraps or ⅛ yard of star fabric
- Sewing thread to match your background fabric

Tools

ROTARY CUTTER, RULER + MAT

When cutting your fabric, a rotary cutter, a 6″ × 24″ acrylic ruler and a cutting mat at least 24″ long are essential. These tools will give you the most accurate cutting.

MARKING TOOL

It is helpful to mark your strips so you know which way is up. I suggest using a tailor's chalk pencil. (Don't worry, I'll tell you as we progress when and how to mark your strips.)

LARGE TRAY

As you cut and sew your strips, you'll need to keep them in order from left to right. I find that a large tray or cookie sheet is helpful to organize and carry the whole set of strips from cutting table to sewing machine.

Tips for Cutting Accurately

Make sure your rotary cutter blade is sharp. But be careful: these things are seriously 360 degrees of razor-sharp. Always cut away from yourself and keep your fingers clear of the blade. Cut a few practice pieces if you need to get the hang of using the rotary cutter. Use a gentler touch on the rotary cutter and heavier pressure on the ruler to keep it from shifting. Use the marks on your acrylic ruler to measure (not the marks on the self-healing mat) for the most accurate cuts.

Tips for Sewing Small Patchwork

The sewing of the Constellation Blocks is simple and straightforward, but the patchwork to create the star pieces is quite small. To get the best results, when sewing the seams for your Constellation Block, use a ¼″ seam allowance.

Using the ¼″ foot on your sewing machine can be helpful, but double check with a seam gauge or ruler that your needle is set to sew a precise ¼″ seam. This will ensure that your finished block is the correct size.

When assembling blocks, use a small stitch length like 1.8, to keep the seams secure and prevent them from pulling apart.

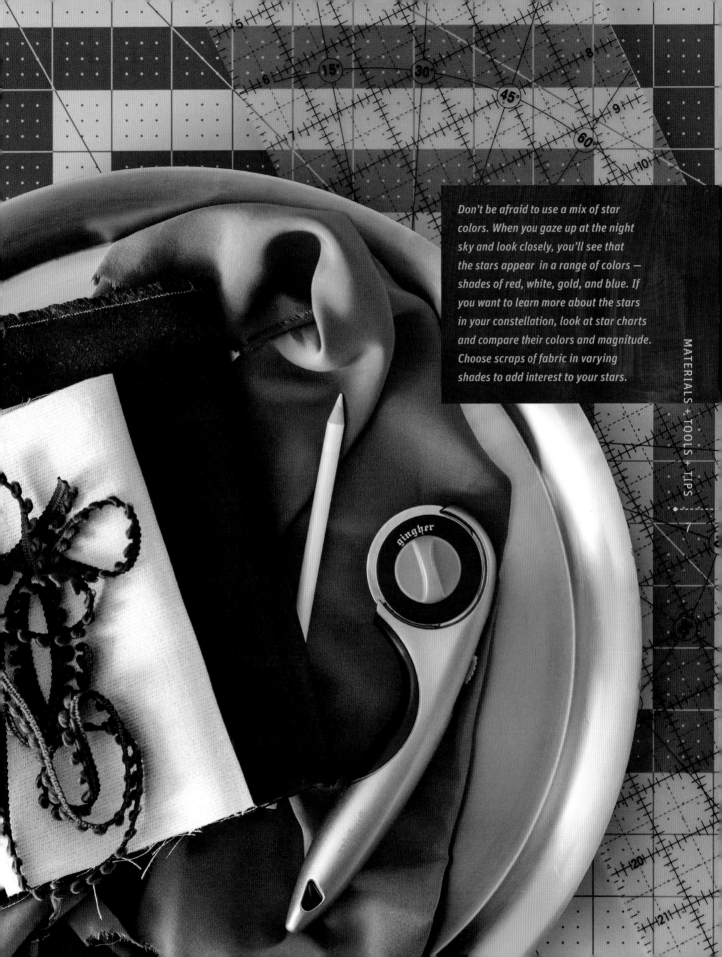

Don't be afraid to use a mix of star colors. When you gaze up at the night sky and look closely, you'll see that the stars appear in a range of colors — shades of red, white, gold, and blue. If you want to learn more about the stars in your constellation, look at star charts and compare their colors and magnitude. Choose scraps of fabric in varying shades to add interest to your stars.

ARIES

OPTIMISTIC + COURAGEOUS + CONFIDENT

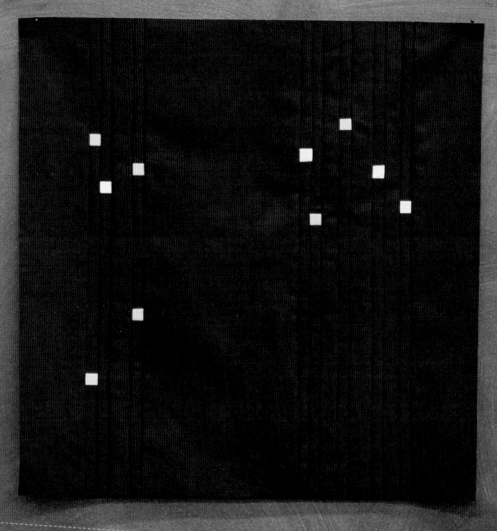

CUTTING

- From the background fabric, cut:
  - (1) 7½″ × 21″ strip
  - (2) 4″ × 21″ strips
  - (2) 1½″ × 21″ strips
  - (2) 1¼″ × 21″ strips
  - (8) 1″ × 21″ strips

- From the star fabric(s), cut:
  - (10) 1″ squares

ASSEMBLING

1. Arrange the (8) 1″ × 21″ strips of background fabric on a flat surface such as a large tray. Set aside the other strips.

2. Using a tailor's chalk pencil, mark one end of each of the strips. This will always be the top of the strip.

3. Working with your first strip and using your chalk pencil, draw a horizontal line across the width of the strip at the two measurements indicated in the chart below (right).

4. Using your rotary cutter and a ruler, cut across the two marks from Step 3 and place the three pieces of segmented strip back, in order, on your flat surface.

5. Repeat Step 4 for the remaining strips.

6. Working with your first strip, sew star squares between the two cuts from Step 4.

Press the seams away from each star and place the pieced strip back in order on your surface.

7. Repeat for the remaining 7 strips.

8. Referencing the Assembly Diagram, arrange the wider strips and the pieced strips in the order shown.

9. Aligning the top edges, position the first two strips right sides together, and sew along the long side using a ¼″ seam allowance. Continue to assemble each strip in order, but do not press yet. This will help you avoid catching the previous seam allowance in your next seam on the narrower strips.

10. When the assembly is complete, press all the seams to one side and trim your block to the required size for your selected project.

Assembly Diagram

STRIP	CUT
1	5½″ and 15¾″
2	7½″
3	6¾″ and 13″
4	6″
5	8¾″
6	4½″
7	6¾″
8	8¼″

tip

Make sure to keep all the chalk marks at the top and maintain the order of the strips as you sew them. If a strip is accidentally inverted, the stars will be in the wrong position.

April 20 — May 20

TAURUS

RELIABLE + DETERMINED + PATIENT

CUTTING

- From the background fabric, cut:
  (1) 4″ × 21″ strip
  (3) 3¾″ × 21″ strips
  (1) 2¾″ × 21″ strip
  (1) 1½″ × 21″ strip
  (10) 1″ × 21″ strips

- From the star fabric(s), cut:
  (11) 1″ squares

ASSEMBLING

1. Arrange the (10) 1″ × 21″ strips of background fabric on a flat surface such as a large tray. Set aside the other strips.

2. Using a tailor's chalk pencil, mark one end of each of the strips. This will always be the top of the strip.

3. Working with your first strip and using your chalk pencil, draw a horizontal line across the width of the strip at 5¾″ from the top as indicated in the chart below.

4. Using your rotary cutter and a ruler, cut across the mark from Step 3 and place the two pieces of segmented strip back, in order, on your flat surface.

5. Repeat Step 4 for the remaining strips, cutting strip 7 into three segments as indicated on the chart below (right).

6. Working with your first strip, sew a star square between the cut from Step 4. Press both seams away from each star and place the pieced strip back in order on your surface.

7. Repeat for the remaining 9 strips.

8. Referencing the Assembly Diagram, arrange the wider strips and the pieced strips in order from left to right.

9. Aligning the top edges, position the first two strips right sides together, and sew along the long side using a ¼″ seam allowance. Continue to attach each strip in order, but do not press yet. This will help you avoid catching the previous seam allowance in your next seam on the narrower strips.

10. When the assembly is complete, press all the seams to one side and trim your block to the required size for your selected project.

Assembly Diagram

STRIP	CUT
1	5¾″
2	2¾″
3	11″
4	7½″
5	12″
6	10″
7	11½″ and 12½″
8	14¼″
9	17″
10	17½″

tip

Make sure to keep all the chalk marks at the top and maintain the order of the strips as you sew them.

GEMINI

DYNAMIC + WITTY + IDEALISTIC

CUTTING

- From the background fabric, cut:
    - (1) 5¾″ × 21″ strip
    - (1) 4½″ × 21″ strip
    - (1) 2½″ × 21″ strip
    - (1) 2″ × 21″ strip
    - (3) 1½″ × 21″ strips
    - (1) 1¼″ × 21″ strip
    - (10) 1″ × 21″ strips
- From the star fabric(s), cut:
    - (14) 1″ squares

ASSEMBLING

1. Arrange the (10) 1″ × 21″ strips of background fabric on a flat surface such as a large tray. Set aside the other strips.

2. Using a tailor's chalk pencil, mark one end of each of the strips. This will always be the top of the strip.

3. Working with your first strip and using your chalk pencil, draw a horizontal line across the width of the strip at 6½″ from the top as indicated in the chart below (right).

4. Using your rotary cutter and a ruler, cut across the mark from Step 3 and place the two pieces of segmented strip back, in order, on your flat surface.

5. Repeat Step 4 for the remaining strips, cutting strips 5, 7 and 9 into multiple segments as indicated on the chart below.

6. Working with your first strip, sew a star square between the cut from Step 4. Press both seams away from each star and place the pieced strip back in order on your surface.

7. Repeat for the remaining 9 strips.

8. Referencing the Assembly Diagram, arrange the wider strips and the pieced strips in order from left to right.

9. Aligning the top edges, position the first two strips right sides together, and sew along the long side using a ¼″ seam allowance. Continue to attach each strip in order, but do not press yet. This will help you avoid catching the previous seam allowance in your next seam on the narrower strips.

10. When the assembly is complete, press all the seams to one side and trim your block to the required size for your selected project.

Assembly Diagram

STRIP	CUT
1	6½″
2	4½″
3	6″
4	9½″
5	3¼″, 12″, and 17¼″
6	4″
7	6″ and 16″
8	10¼″
9	5″ and 13½″
10	14″

tip

Make sure to keep all the chalk marks at the top and maintain the order of the strips as you sew them.

CANCER

NURTURING + INTUITIVE + PROTECTING

CUTTING

- From the background fabric, cut:
  (2) 6¼″ × 21″ strips   (1) 1¼″ × 21″ strip
  (1) 5¼″ × 21″ strip   (7) 1″ × 21″ strips
  (1) 1½″ × 21″ strip

- From the star fabric(s), cut:
  (7) 1″ squares

ASSEMBLING

1. Arrange the (7) 1″ × 21″ strips of background fabric on a flat surface such as a large tray. Set aside the other strips.

2. Using a tailor's chalk pencil, mark one end of each of the strips. This will always be the top of the strip.

3. Working with your first strip and using your chalk pencil, draw a horizontal line across the width of the strip 3½″ from the top as indicated in the chart below (right).

4. Using your rotary cutter and a ruler, cut across the mark from Step 3 and place the two pieces of segmented strip back, in order, on your flat surface.

5. Repeat Step 4 for the remaining 6 strips.

6. Working with your first strip, sew a star fabric square between the cut from Step 4.

Press both seams away from the star and place the pieced strip back in order on your flat surface.

7. Repeat for the remaining 6 strips.

8. Referencing the Assembly Diagram, arrange the wider strips and the pieced strips in order from left to right.

9. Aligning the top edges, position the first two strips right sides together, and sew along the long side using a ¼″ seam allowance. Continue to attach each strip in order, but do not press yet. This will help you avoid catching the previous seam allowance in your next seam on the narrower strips.

10. When the assembly is complete, press all the seams to one side and trim your block to the required size for your selected project.

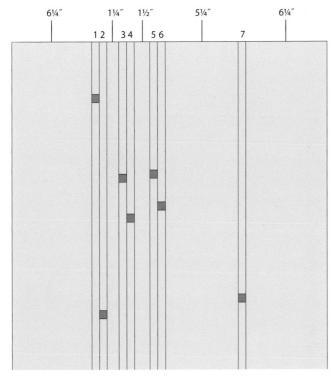

Assembly Diagram

STRIP	CUT
1	3½″
2	17″
3	8½″
4	11″
5	8¼″
6	10¼″
7	16″

tip

Make sure to keep all the chalk marks at the top and maintain the order of the strips as you sew them.

LEO

ENTHUSIASTIC + GENEROUS + MAGNANIMOUS

CUTTING

- From the background fabric, cut:
  - (1) 5½″ × 21″ strip
  - (2) 4¼″ × 21″ strips
  - (1) 3¾″ × 21″ strip
  - (1) 1¾″ × 21″ strip
  - (9) 1″ × 21″ strips

- From the star fabric(s), cut:
  - (9) 1″ squares

ASSEMBLING

1. Arrange the (9) 1″ × 21″ strips of background fabric on a flat surface such as a large tray. Set aside the other strips.

2. Using a tailor's chalk pencil, mark one end of each of the strips. This will be the top of the strip.

3. Working with your first strip and using your chalk pencil, draw a horizontal line across the width of the strip at 14½″ from the top as indicated in the chart below (right).

4. Using your rotary cutter and a ruler, cut across the mark from Step 3 and place the two pieces of segmented strip back, in order, on your flat surface.

5. Repeat Step 4 for the remaining 8 strips.

6. Working with your first strip, sew a star square between the cut from Step 4. Press both seams away from the star and place the pieced strip back in order on your surface.

7. Repeat for the remaining 8 strips.

8. Referencing the Assembly Diagram, arrange the wider strips and the pieced strips in order from left to right.

9. Aligning the top edges, position the first two strips right sides together, and sew along the long side using a ¼″ seam allowance. Continue to attach each strip in order, but do not press yet. This will help you avoid catching the previous seam allowance in your next seam on the narrower strips.

10. When the assembly is complete, press all the seams to one side and trim your block to the required size for your selected project.

Assembly Diagram

STRIP	CUT
1	14½″
2	10½″
3	13″
4	6¾″
5	8½″
6	4¼″
7	9½″
8	12″
9	5″

tip

Make sure to keep all the chalk marks at the top and maintain the order of the strips as you sew them.

VIRGO

MODEST + PRACTICAL + RELIABLE

CUTTING

- From the background fabric, cut:
  - (2) 4¾″ × 21″ strips
  - (2) 2¼″ × 21″ strips
  - (3) 1½″ × 21″ strips
  - (2) 1¼″ × 21″ strips
  - (10) 1″ × 21″ strips

- From the star fabric(s), cut:
  - (12) 1″ squares

ASSEMBLING

1. Arrange the (10) 1″ × 21″ strips of background fabric on a flat surface such as a large tray. Set aside the other strips.

2. Using a tailor's chalk pencil, mark one end of each of the strips. This will always be the top of the strip.

3. Working with your first strip and using your chalk pencil, draw a horizontal line across the width of the strip 13″ from the top as indicated in the chart below (right).

4. Using your rotary cutter and a ruler, cut across the mark from Step 3 and place the two pieces of segmented strip back, in order, on your flat surface.

5. Repeat Step 4 for the remaining strips, cutting strips 3 and 6 into multiple segments as indicated.

6. Working with your first strip, sew a star square between the cut from Step 4. Press both seams away from the star and place the pieced strip back in order on your surface.

7. Repeat for the remaining 9 strips.

8. Referencing the Assembly Diagram, arrange the wider strips and the pieced strips in order from left to right.

9. Aligning the top edges, position the first two strips right sides together, and sew along the long side using a ¼″ seam allowance. Continue to attach each strip in order, but do not press yet. This will help you avoid catching the previous seam allowance in your next seam on the narrower strips.

10. When the assembly is complete, press all the seams to one side and trim your block to the required size for your selected project.

Assembly Diagram

STRIP	CUT
1	13″
2	15″
3	11½″ and 14¼″
4	11″
5	6¼″
6	8″ and 13½″
7	11½″
8	8¾″
9	7½″
10	5¼″

tip

Make sure to keep all the chalk marks at the top and maintain the order of the strips as you sew them.

LIBRA

CHARMING + GRACIOUS + DIPLOMATIC

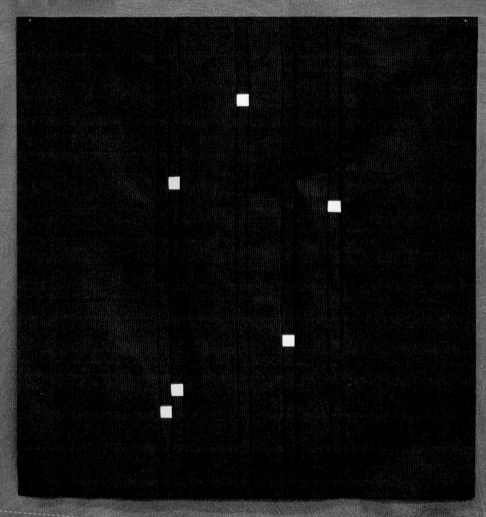

CUTTING

- From the background fabric, cut:
  - (2) 7¼″ × 21″ strips
  - (1) 3″ × 21″ strip
  - (2) 2″ × 21″ strips
  - (5) 1″ × 21″ strips

- From the star fabric(s), cut:
  - (6) 1″ squares

ASSEMBLING

1. Arrange the (5) 1″ × 21″ strips of background fabric on a flat surface such as a large tray. Set aside the other strips.

2. Using a tailor's chalk pencil, mark one end of each of the strips. This will always be the top of the strip.

3. Working with your first strip and using your chalk pencil, draw a horizontal line across the width of the strip 17″ from the top as indicated in the chart below (right).

4. Using your rotary cutter and a ruler, cut across the mark from Step 3 and place the two pieces of segmented strip back, in order, on your flat surface.

5. Repeat Step 4 for the remaining strips, cutting strip 2 into mutliple segments.

6. Working with your first strip, sew a star square between the cut from Step 4. Press both seams away from the star and place the pieced strip back in order on your surface.

7. Repeat for the remaining 4 strips.

8. Referencing the Assembly Diagram, arrange the wider strips and the pieced strips in order from left to right.

9. Aligning the top edges, position the first two strips right sides together, and sew along the long side using a ¼″ seam allowance. Continue to attach each strip in order, but do not press yet. This will help you avoid catching the previous seam allowance in your next seam on the narrower strips.

10. When the assembly is complete, press all the seams to one side and trim your block to the required size for your selected project.

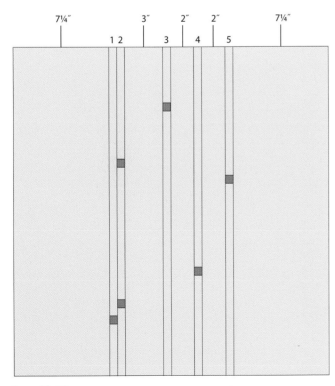

Assembly Diagram

STRIP	CUT
1	17″
2	7¼″ and 16″
3	3¾″
4	14″
5	8¼″

tip

Make sure to keep all the chalk marks at the top and maintain the order of the strips as you sew them.

SCORPIO

MYSTERIOUS + PASSIONATE + MAGNETIC

CUTTING

- From the background fabric, cut:

  (2) 4¼″ × 21″ strips   (1) 1¾″ × 21″ strip

  (1) 2¼″ × 21″ strip   (2) 1¼″ × 21″ strips

  (2) 2″ × 21″ strips   (13) 1″ × 21″ strips

- From the star fabric(s), cut:

  (16) 1″ squares

ASSEMBLING

1. Arrange the (13) 1″ × 21″ strips of background fabric on a flat surface such as a large tray. Set aside the other strips.

2. Using a tailor's chalk pencil, mark one end of each of the strips. This will always be the top of the strip.

3. Working with your first strip and using your chalk pencil, draw a horizontal line across the width of the strip 13½″ from the top as indicated in the chart below (right).

4. Using your rotary cutter and a ruler, cut across the mark from Step 3 and place the two pieces of segmented strip back, in order, on your flat surface.

5. Repeat Step 4 for the remaining strips, cutting strips 4, 8 and 13 into multiple segments.

6. Working with your first strip, sew a star square between the cut from Step 4. Press both seams away from the star and place the pieced strip back in order on your surface.

7. Repeat for the remaining 12 strips.

8. Referencing the Assembly Diagram, arrange the wider strips and the pieced strips in order from left to right.

9. Aligning the top edges, position the first two strips right sides together, and sew along the long side using a ¼″ seam allowance. Continue to attach each strip in order, but do not press yet. This will help you avoid catching the previous seam allowance in your next seam on the narrower strips.

10. When the assembly is complete, press all the seams to one side and trim your block to the required size for your selected project.

Assembly Diagram

STRIP	CUT
1	13½″
2	15¼″
3	14½″
4	13¼″ and 16¾″
5	13½″
6	16½″
7	16″
8	11½″ and 13½″
9	8″
10	7″
11	6¾″
12	3½″
13	5″ and 7″

tip

Make sure to keep all the chalk marks at the top and maintain the order of the strips while sewing.

November 22 — December 21

SAGITTARIUS

INDEPENDENT + HONEST + ADVENTUROUS

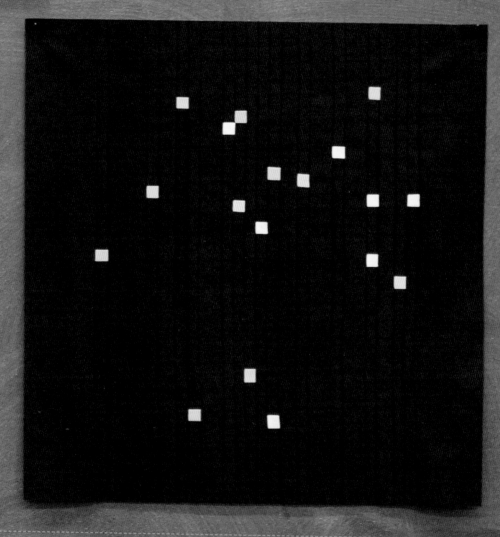

CUTTING

- From the background fabric, cut:
  (2) 4¼″ × 21″ strips
  (1) 2¼″ × 21″ strip
  (3) 1½″ × 21″ strips
  (3) 1¼″ × 21″ strips
  (14) 1″ × 21″ strips

- From the star fabric(s), cut:
  (18) 1″ squares

ASSEMBLING

1. Arrange the (14) 1″ × 21″ strips of background fabric on a flat surface such as a large tray. Set aside the other strips.

2. Using a tailor's chalk pencil, mark one end of each of the strips. This will always be the top of the strip.

3. Working with your first strip and using your chalk pencil, draw a horizontal line across the width of the strip 10¼″ from the top as indicated in the chart below (right).

4. Using your rotary cutter and a ruler, cut across the mark from Step 3 and place the two pieces of segmented strip back, in order, on your flat surface.

5. Repeat Step 4 for the remaining strips, cutting strips 6, 9 and 12 into multiple segments.

6. Working with your first strip, sew a star square between the cut from Step 4. Press both seams away from the star and place the pieced strip back in order on your surface.

7. Repeat for the remaining 13 strips.

8. Referencing the Assembly Diagram, arrange the wider strips and the pieced strips in order from left to right.

9. Aligning the top edges, position the first two strips right sides together, and sew along the long side using a ¼″ seam allowance. Continue to attach each strip in order, but do not press yet. This will help you avoid catching the previous seam allowance in your next seam on the narrower strips.

10. When the assembly is complete, press all the seams to one side and trim your block to the required size for your selected project.

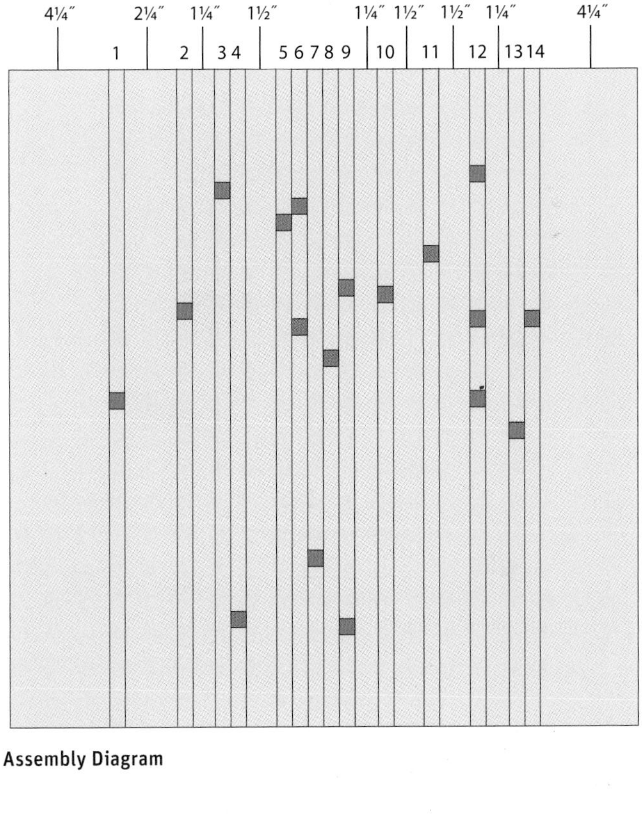

Assembly Diagram

STRIP	CUT
1	10¼″
2	7½″
3	3¾″
4	17″
5	4¾″
6	4¼″ and 8″
7	15¼″
8	9″
9	6¾″ and 17¼″
10	7″
11	5¾″
12	3¼″, 7¾″, and 10¼″
13	11¼″
14	7¾″

tip

Make sure to keep all the chalk marks at the top and maintain the order of the strips as you sew them.

CAPRICORN

PRACTICAL + DISCIPLINED + AMBITIOUS

CUTTING

- From the background fabric, cut:
  - (2) 4″ × 21″ strips
  - (3) 2¾″ × 21″ strips
  - (1) 2¼″ × 21″ strip
  - (1) 1½″ × 21″ strip
  - (10) 1″ × 21″ strips
- From the star fabric(s), cut:
  - (11) 1″ squares

ASSEMBLING

1. Arrange the (10) 1″ × 21″ strips of background fabric on a flat surface such as a large tray. Set aside the other strips.

2. Using a tailor's chalk pencil, mark one end of each of the strips. This will always be the top of the strip.

3. Working with your first strip and using your chalk pencil, draw a horizontal line across the width of the strip 7¼″ from the top as indicated in the chart below.

4. Using your rotary cutter and a ruler, cut across the mark from Step 3 and place the two pieces of segmented strip back, in order, on your flat surface.

5. Repeat Step 4 for the remaining strips, cutting strip 10 into multiple segments.

6. Working with your first strip, sew a star square between the cut from Step 4. Press both seams away from the star and place the pieced strip back in order on your surface.

7. Repeat for the remaining 9 strips.

8. Referencing the Assembly Diagram, arrange the wider strips and the pieced strips in order from left to right.

9. Aligning the top edges, position the first two strips right sides together, and sew along the long side using a ¼″ seam allowance. Continue to attach each strip in order, but do not press yet. This will help you avoid catching the previous seam allowance in your next seam on the narrower strips.

10. When the assembly is complete, press all the seams to one side and trim your block to the required size for your selected project.

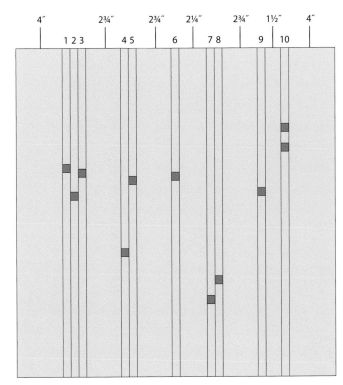

Assembly Diagram

STRIP	CUT
1	7¼″
2	9″
3	7½″
4	12½″
5	8″
6	7¾″
7	15½″
8	14¼″
9	8¾″
10	4¾″ and 6″

tip

Make sure to keep all the chalk marks at the top and maintain the order of the strips as you sew them.

ΔQUΔRIUS

FRIENDLY + CREATIVE + INTELLECTUAL

CUTTING

- From the background fabric, cut:
  - (1) 4¾″ × 21″ strip
  - (2) 4″ × 21″ strips
  - (1) 2″ × 21″ strip
  - (1) 1¾″ × 21″ strip
  - (2) 1¼″ × 21″ strips
  - (12) 1″ × 21″ strips

- From the star fabric(s), cut:
  - (14) 1″ squares

ASSEMBLING

1. Arrange the (12) 1″ × 21″ strips of background fabric on a flat surface such as a large tray. Set aside the other strips.

2. Using a tailor's chalk pencil, mark one end of each of the strips. This will always be the top of the strip.

3. Working with your first strip and using your chalk pencil, draw a horizontal line across the width of the strip 10″ from the top as indicated in the chart below.

4. Using your rotary cutter and a ruler, cut across the mark from Step 3 and place the two pieces of segmented strip back, in order, on your flat surface.

5. Repeat Step 4 for the remaining strips, cutting strips 4 and 5 into multiple sections.

6. Working with your first strip, sew a star square between the cut from Step 4. Press both seams away from the star and place the pieced strip back in order on your surface.

7. Repeat for the remaining 11 strips.

8. Referencing the Assembly Diagram, arrange the wider strips and the pieced strips in order from left to right.

9. Aligning the top edges, position the first two strips right sides together, and sew along the long side using a ¼″ seam allowance. Continue to attach each strip in order, but do not press yet. This will help you avoid catching the previous seam allowance in your next seam on the narrower strips.

10. When the assembly is complete, press all the seams to one side and trim your block to the required size for your selected project.

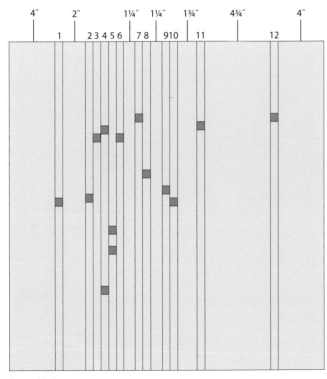

Assembly Diagram

STRIP	CUT
1	10″
2	9¾″
3	6″
4	5½″ and 15½″
5	11¾″ and 13″
6	6″
7	4¾″
8	8¼″
9	9¼″
10	10″
11	5¼″
12	4¾″

tip

Make sure to keep all the chalk marks at the top and maintain the order of the strips as you sew them.

PISCES

IMAGINATIVE + COMPASSIONATE + INTUITIVE

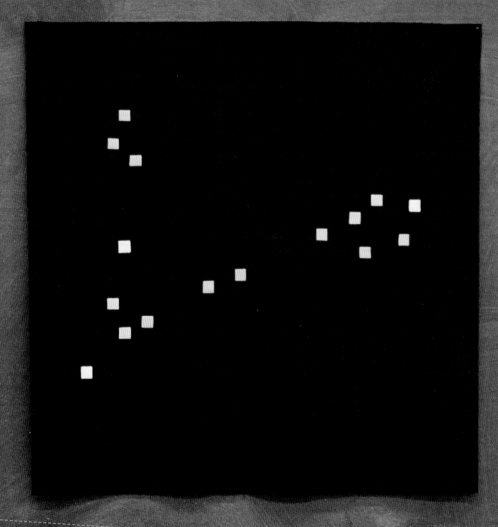

CONSTELLATIONS

30

CUTTING

- From the background fabric, cut:

  (3) 3¾″ × 21″ strips   (2) 1¼″ × 21″ strips

  (1) 2¼″ × 21″ strip   (13) 1″ × 21″ strips

  (2) 1½″ × 21″ strips

- From the star fabric(s), cut:

  (16) 1″ squares

ASSEMBLING

1. Arrange the (13) 1″ × 21″ strips of background fabric on a flat surface such as a large tray. Set aside the other strips.

2. Using a tailor's chalk pencil, mark one end of each of the strips. This will always be the top of the strip.

3. Working with your first strip and using your chalk pencil, draw a horizontal line across the width of the strip 15½″ from the top as indicated in the chart below.

4. Using your rotary cutter and a ruler, cut across the mark from Step 3 and place the two pieces of segmented strip back, in order, on your flat surface.

5. Repeat Step 4 for the remaining strips, cutting strips 2 and 3 into multiple segments.

6. Working with your first strip, sew a star square between the cut from Step 4. Press both seams away from the star and place the pieced strip back in order on your surface.

7. Repeat for the remaining 12 strips.

8. Referencing the Assembly Diagram, arrange the wider strips and the pieced strips in order from left to right.

9. Aligning the top edges, position the first two strips right sides together, and sew along the long side using a ¼″ seam allowance. Continue to attach each strip in order, but do not press yet. This will help you avoid catching the previous seam allowance in your next seam on the narrower strips.

10. When the assembly is complete, press all the seams to one side and trim your block to the required size for your selected project.

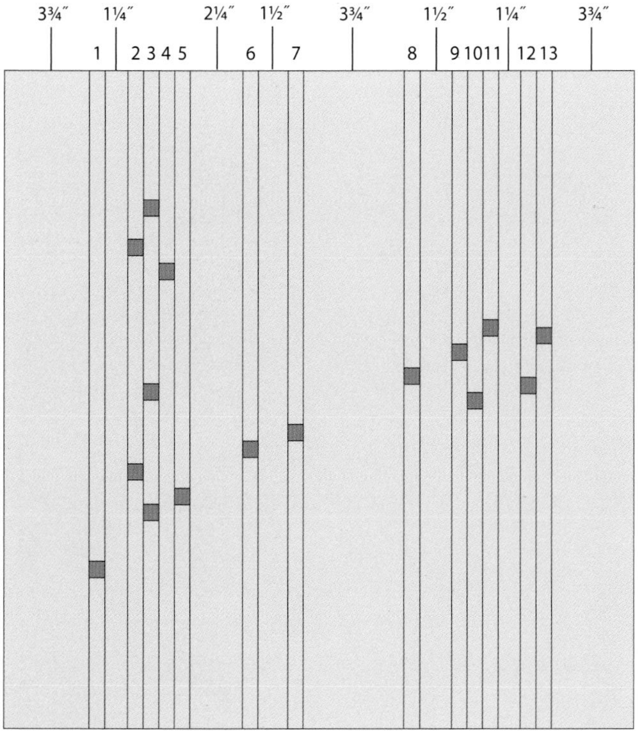

Assembly Diagram

STRIP	CUT
1	15½″
2	5½″ and 12½″
3	4¼″, 10″, and 13¾″
4	6¼″
5	13¼″
6	11¾″
7	11¼″
8	9½″
9	8¾″
10	10¼″
11	8″
12	9¾″
13	8¼″

tip

Make sure to keep all the chalk marks at the top and maintain the order of the strips as you sew them.

The Hunter

ORION

One of the most widely recognized and beloved constellations in the night sky, Orion is visible throughout the world and a favorite of star-gazers. Most cultures have a myth associated with the constellation. In some places, the stars illustrate a hunter, elsewhere a shepherd.

CUTTING

- From the background fabric, cut:
  - (2) 4¾″ × 21″ strips
  - (2) 2¼″ × 21″ strips
  - (2) 1¾″ × 21″ strips
  - (2) 1¼″ × 21″ strips
  - (11) 1″ × 21″ strips
- From the star fabric(s), cut:
  - (18) 1″ squares

ASSEMBLING

1. Arrange the (11) 1″ × 21″ strips of background fabric on a flat surface such as a large tray. Set aside the other strips.

2. Using a tailor's chalk pencil, mark one end of each of the strips. This will always be the top of the strip.

3. Working with your first strip and using your chalk pencil, draw two horizontal lines across the width of the strip at the measurements indicated in the chart below (right).

4. Using your rotary cutter and a ruler, cut across the marks from Step 3 and place the three pieces of segmented strip back, in order, on your flat surface.

5. Repeat Step 4 for the remaining strips.

6. Working with your first strip, sew star squares between the cuts from Step 4.

7. Press all of the seams away from the two stars and place the pieced strip back in order on your flat surface.

8. Repeat for the remaining 10 strips.

9. Referencing the Assembly Diagram, arrange the wider strips and the pieced strips in order from left to right.

10. Aligning the top edges, position the first two strips right sides together, and sew along the long side using a ¼″ seam allowance. Continue to attach each strip in order, but do not press yet. This will help you avoid catching the previous seam allowance in your next seam on the narrower strips.

11. When the assembly is complete, press all the seams to one side and trim your block to the required size for your selected project.

Assembly Diagram

STRIP	CUT
1	3½″ and 6½″
2	6″
3	8¼″
4	9″
5	6¾″
6	8″ and 12¾″
7	12¼″ and 17″
8	11¾″
9	4″
10	4¾″, 9″, and 14¼″
11	5½″, 8″, and 14¾″

tip

Make sure to keep all the chalk marks at the top and maintain the order of the strips as you sew them.

PART 2

THE PROJECTS

These minimal star blocks can be made into plenty of stunningly modern projects. Make a quilt for your family with a block for each family member's star sign. Stitch up a jacket or tote to show off your zodiac. A silky cloth for tarot readings makes a great gift for your favorite witchy woman. Here are eight projects to inspire you, but you can also create your own— upholster the cushions of your dining chairs or make starry curtains for a child's room. Let your imagination run wild as you plan the perfect project for your twinkling patchwork!

Finished Size: 90″ × 90″

TWELVE CONSTELLATION QUILT

DESIGNED BY AMBER CORCORAN

All the astrological constellations are represented in this celestial wonder. Like a window to a sky full of stars, this quilt captures the night sky and brings it right into your home! Maybe make the blocks over the course of a year, finishing each constellation during the month of the astrological sign. In this quilt, blocks are spaced apart with additional background fabric, giving each a bit of room to stand out.

I suggest using a mix of shades of star fabrics for a twinkling effect. For this quilt, I looked at charts with star magnitudes notated and chose my brightest fabrics to be the brightest stars. Did you know that stars emit different colors of light? If you want to get astronomically exact, you could choose star fabrics in pale muted shades of white, yellow, red and blue — all the hues that stars come in!

MATERIALS

- 9½ yards background fabric
- ¼ yard or mix of scraps for stars
- 8¼ yards backing fabric
- ¾ yard binding fabric
- 96″ × 96″ batting

CUTTING

For the Constellation Blocks, cut the background and star fabrics according to each block's specifications (see pages 8–33).

From the remaining background fabric, cut:
  (8) 5½″ × 20½″ rectangles
  (4) 10½″ × 20½″ rectangles
  (7) 3½″ × WOF (Width Of Fabric) strips

From the binding fabric, cut:
  (10) 2½″ × WOF strips

tip

You may decide that you want to swap one of the astrological blocks with Orion (see page 32) or perhaps feature a single block on the backing. Either way, this setting allows for a total of 12 blocks to be incorporated in the quilt top.

tip

If you'd like to follow my arrangement, I placed (from left to right) Capricorn, Aquarius, and Pisces in Row 1; Aries, Taurus, and Gemini in Row 2; Cancer, Leo, and Virgo in Row 3; and Libra, Scorpio, and Sagittarius in Row 4. A full-sized photograph of this quilt is shown on the cover of this book.

quilting tip

For this quilt, contrasting thread color connects the stars in each constellation (see page 74 for the quilting diagrams). A matching thread quilts simple horizontal lines to give the quilt more structure. If you are new to quilting, visit, www.luckyspool.com, and download their free Quiltmaking Basics PDF.

ASSEMBLING

Note: Use a ¼" seam allowance when assembling this project.

1. Referencing pages 8–33, assemble the 12 Constellation Blocks and trim each to 20½" square.

2. Sew together the (7) 3½" × WOF strips, end-to-end, then trim to create (3) 3½" × 90" background strips.

3. Referencing the Assembly Diagram (opposite) for placement, lay out your blocks and background rectangles in a pleasing arrangement of 4 rows on a design wall or flat surface. Be sure that each row contains (2) 5½" × 20½" and (1) 10½" × 20½" background rectangles and 3 Constellation Blocks. Position a 90" background strip below Rows 1, 2, and 3.

4. Assemble the quilt top by piecing together one row at a time. Sew the background rectangles and Constellation Blocks together in order from left to right. Press the seams to one side.

5. Gather your assembled background strips from Step 2. Sew the rows and background strips in this order: Row 1, background strip, Row 2, background strip, Row 3, background strip, Row 4. Press all of the seams to one side.

6. Layer the backing fabric, batting and quilt top. Baste and quilt as desired. Attach the binding using your favorite method.

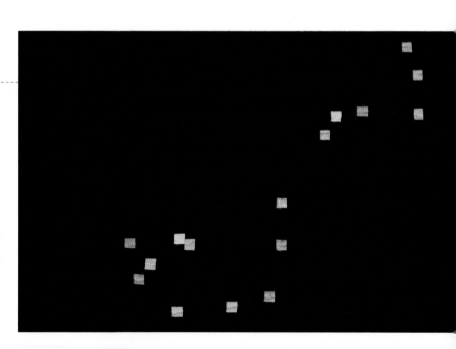

5½″ × 20½″   5½″ × 20½″   10½″ × 20½″

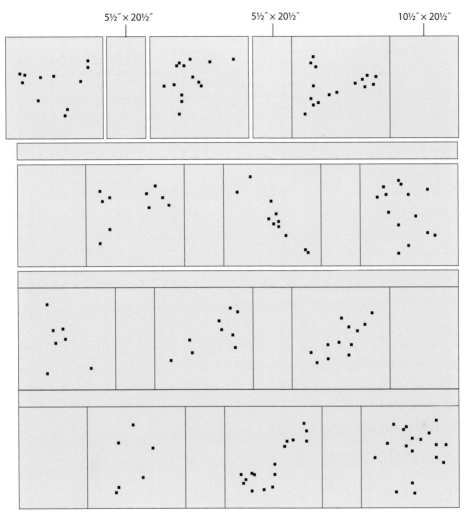

Assembly Diagram

Finished Quilt Sizes:

Baby (1 block): 36″ × 40″ • Throw (1–6 blocks): 60″ × 60″

Twin (1–9 blocks): 70″ × 90″ • Full/Queen (1–9 blocks): 90″ × 90″

King (1–9 blocks): 110″ × 110″

MIX-AND-MATCH
ASTROLOGICAL QUILT

DESIGNED BY AMBER CORCORAN

These quilts are a personalizable, choose-your-own-adventure kind of project. You decide which of five quilt top sizes to make featuring between one and nine Block Constellations. You might decide to make a two-block quilt for a wedding or anniversary gift, or create a quilt with a single block to celebrate a new baby, or to give to a loved one headed off to college. A quilt including a block for each member of your family, large or small, is perfect for cuddling up on the couch.

No matter how many blocks are needed for your mix-and-match quilt, the end result is sure to be a personal keepsake. Before you sew your blocks together, consider taking the customization one step further by embroidering a name or date onto each block. The arrangements on the following pages will show you how to join up to nine blocks together into a quilt of any size, to celebrate the folks in your life.

Baby Quilt

MATERIALS

- 1⅝ yards background fabric
- ⅛ yard or mix of scraps for stars
- 1¼ yards backing fabric
- ½ yard binding fabric
- 42″ × 46″ batting

CUTTING

For the Constellation Block, cut the background and star fabrics according to the appropriate block's specifications.

From the remaining background fabric, cut:
(2) 20½″ × 8½″ rectangles
(2) 36½″ × 10½″ rectangles

From the binding fabric, cut:
(5) 2½″ × WOF strips

ASSEMBLING

1. Referencing pages 8–33, assemble your chosen Constellation Block and trim to 20½″ square.

2. Using a ¼″ seam allowance, sew a 20½″ × 8½″ rectangle to the left and right sides of an assembled Constellation Block. Press the seams to one side.

3. Referencing the Assembly Diagram below, sew a 36½″ × 10½″ rectangle to the top and to the bottom of the assembled unit from Step 2. Press the seams to one side.

FINISHING

Layer the backing fabric, batting and quilt top. Baste and quilt as desired. Attach the binding using your favorite method. The sample quilt on the previous page uses Star Stitch Quilt Tying Technique (see page 76).

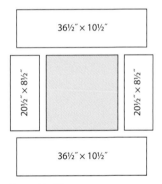

Assembly Diagram

tip

Pin a scrap of paper with the dimensions to each background fabric piece to help you assemble later.

tip

If you are new to quilt making, go to the Lucky Spool website, www.luckyspool.com, and download the free Quiltmaking Basics PDF.

Calculating Yardage for the Throw, Twin, Queen + King Quilts

BACKGROUND FABRIC

Calculate the background fabric yardage once you decide on the number of blocks and size of your quilt top. These larger sizes require anywhere from 3⅞ yards to 13 yards of non-directional background fabric. The fabric requirements for the Panels also include what you will need for your Constellation Blocks.

First, select the quilt option (see pages 44-45). Next, choose from one to three Panels (see page 44) based on the number of blocks you are including. Finally, add up the required background fabric amounts listed for your chosen Panels and the quilt option you chose.

For the Example below, if you want to create a queen-size quilt with four Constellation Blocks, you could make a one-block Panel (Panel A) and a three-block Panel (Panel C). using the #2 Queen layout.

This is how it would add up: (Panel A) 2 yards + (Panel C) 2½ yards + (Queen #2) 4 yards = 8½ yards total background fabric.

EXAMPLE

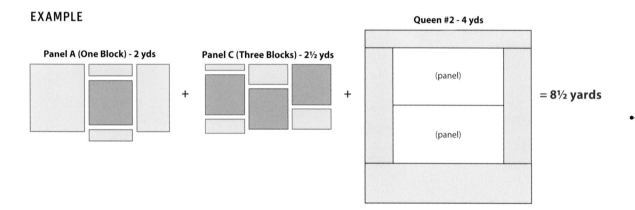

Panel A (One Block) - 2 yds

Panel C (Three Blocks) - 2½ yds

Queen #2 - 4 yds

(panel)

(panel)

= 8½ yards

BACKING, BINDING + BATTING

	BACKING FABRIC	BINDING FABRIC	BATTING
THROW	3⅞ yards	⅝ yard	66″ × 66″
TWIN	5½ yards	¾ yard	76″ × 96″
QUEEN	8¼ yards	⅞ yard	96″ × 96″
KING	9⅞ yards	1 yard	116″ × 116″

STARS

⅛ yard of fabric should be plenty for all of your star squares or use a mix of scraps for the stars instead.

tip

Are there multiple Scorpios in your family? A set or two of Gemini twins? Consider rotating the identical blocks in your quilt layout to add variation when you have recurring signs. There really is no up or down in the night sky.

The Panels

Panel A (One Block) - 2 yds
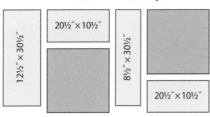

25½″ × 30½″

20½″ × 5½″

15½″ × 30½″

20½″ × 5½″

Panel B (Two Blocks) - 2¼ yds

20½″ × 10½″

12½″ × 30½″

8½″ × 30½″

20½″ × 10½″

Panel C (Three Blocks) - 2½ yds
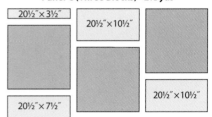

20½″ × 3½″

20½″ × 10½″

20½″ × 7½″

20½″ × 10½″

Twin, Queen, King + Throw Quilt Options

44

TWIN QUILTS

Twin #1

(2) 20½″ × WOF strips; sewn together, end-to-end, then subcut to (1) 70½″ × 20½″

5½″ × 30½″

(2) 5½″ × WOF strips, subcut to (2) 5½″ × 30½″

(panel)

5½″ × 30½″

(1) 70½″ × WOF strip; trim to (1) 70½″ × 40½″

fabric needed: 3⅔ yds

Twin #2

70½″ × 10½″

5½″ × 60½″

(2) 10½″ × WOF strips; sewn together, end-to-end, then subcut to (1) 70½″ × 10½″

(panel)

(3) 5½″ × WOF strips, sewn together, end-to-end, then subcut to (2) 5½″ × 60½″

5½″ × 60½″

(panel)

(2) 20½″ × WOF strips; sewn together, end-to-end, then subcut to (1) 70½″ × 20½″

fabric needed: 2⅓ yds

Twin #3

(panel)

5½″ × 90½″

(5) 5½″ × WOF strips; sewn together, end-to-end, then subcut to (2) 5½″ × 90½″

5½″ × 90½″

(panel)

(panel)

fabric needed: 1 yd

QUEEN QUILTS

Queen #1

(3) 20½″ × WOF strips; sewn together, end-to-end, then subcut to (1) 90½″ × 20½″

15½″ × 30½″

(2) 15½″ × WOF strips, subcut to (2) 15½″ × 30½″

(panel)

15½″ × 30½″

(1) 90½″ × WOF strip, subcut to (1) 90½″ × 40½″

fabric needed: 5¼ yds

Queen #2

(panel)

15½″ × 60½″

(3) 15½″ × WOF strips; sewn together, end-to-end, then subcut to (2) 15½″ × 60½″

15½″ × 60½″

(panel)

(1) 90½″ × WOF strip, subcut to
(1) 90½″ × 10½″ (top)
and (1) 90½″ × 20½″ (bottom)

fabric needed: 4 yds

Queen #3

(panel)

15½″ × 90½″

(5) 15½″ × WOF strips; sewn together, end-to-end, then subcut to (2) 15½″ × 90½″

15½″ × 90½″

(panel)

(panel)

fabric needed: 2½ yds

KING QUILTS

King #1

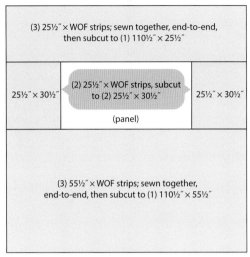

(3) 25½″ × WOF strips; sewn together, end-to-end, then subcut to (1) 110½″ × 25½″

25½″ × 30½″

(2) 25½″ × WOF strips, subcut to (2) 25½″ × 30½″

(panel)

25½″ × 30½″

(3) 55½″ × WOF strips; sewn together, end-to-end, then subcut to (1) 110½″ × 55½″

fabric needed: 8⅓ yds

King #2

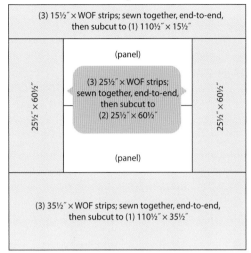

(3) 15½″ × WOF strips; sewn together, end-to-end, then subcut to (1) 110½″ × 15½″

(panel)

25½″ × 60½″

(3) 25½″ × WOF strips; sewn together, end-to-end, then subcut to (2) 25½″ × 60½″

25½″ × 60½″

(panel)

(3) 35½″ × WOF strips; sewn together, end-to-end, then subcut to (1) 110½″ × 35½″

fabric needed: 6½ yds

King #3

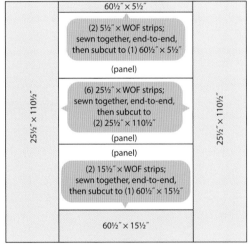

60½″ × 5½″

(2) 5½″ × WOF strips; sewn together, end-to-end, then subcut to (1) 60½″ × 5½″

(panel)

25½″ × 110½″

(6) 25½″ × WOF strips; sewn together, end-to-end, then subcut to (2) 25½″ × 110½″

(panel)

25½″ × 110½″

(panel)

(2) 15½″ × WOF strips; sewn together, end-to-end, then subcut to (1) 60½″ × 15½″

60½″ × 15½″

fabric needed: 5⅝ yds

THROW QUILTS

Throw #1

60½″ × 15½″

(1) 60½″ × WOF strip, subcut to (2) 60½″ × 15½″

(panel)

60½″ × 15½″

fabric needed: 2 yds

Throw #2

(panel)

(panel)

no additional fabric needed

CUTTING AND ASSEMBLING

1. Assemble your chosen Constellation Block(s) and trim to 20½″ square.

2. Cut all of the background fabric to the measurements indicated in the diagrams.

3. Using a ¼″ seam allowance, sew the appropriate Panel(s) for your selected quilt option. Press all of the seams to one side.

4. Once you have your Panel(s) completed, piece together each row, referencing the corresponding quilt diagram on these two pages. Assemble the quilt top by sewing the rows together as shown. Note that all of the #3 quilts are sewn in columns instead of rows. Press all of the seams to one side and finish using the instructions on page 42.

Finished Size: 40″ × 20″

CELESTIAL TABLE RUNNER

DESIGNED BY AMBER CORCORAN

Adorn your table with a bit of magic! This star-strewn table runner will dress up your dining table for any occasion. Handmade tassels are simple, fun to make, and add a timeless sophistication to your project. Choose one or two constellation blocks, and make a beautiful centerpiece to gather around with friends and family.

MATERIALS

- 1½ yards background fabric
- ⅛ yard or mix of scraps for stars
- ¾ yard backing fabric
- 2 skeins cotton embroidery floss for tassels

CUTTING

For the Constellation Block(s), cut the background and star fabrics according to each block's specifications (see pages 8–33).

For the single-block design
From the remaining background fabric, cut:
   (2) 11″ × 21″ rectangles

For the single-block or double-block design
From the backing fabric, cut:
   (2) 21″ squares

ASSEMBLING

Note: Use a ½″ seam allowance when assembling this project.

1. Referencing pages 8–33, assemble your chosen Constellation Block(s) and trim to 21″ square.

2. Position the 2 backing squares right sides together and sew along one edge, leaving a 4″ opening at the center of the seam for turning (Fig. A). Press the seam open.

3. For the double-block design, position your two assembled Constellation Blocks right sides together and sew along one edge, then press the seam open. For the single-block design, position a 21″ × 11″ background rectangle and your assembled Constellation Block right sides together and sew along one edge. Sew the remaining 21″ × 11″ background rectangle to the opposite side of the constellation and press the seams to one side. (Fig. B)

4. Make 4 tassels (see page 78).

5. Position your runner top side up. As shown in Figure C, lay a tassel on the fabric at each corner and pin in place. The tassel ends should be pointing inward toward the center of the table runner. The top of the tassel should be about 1″ measured diagonally from the corner of the raw edge. Change the setting on your sewing machine to a very small stitch length. Tack down each tassel with a ⅜″ seam allowance to secure in place.

tip

Stitch slowly when you approach each corner, being careful not to catch the tassels in the seam as you sew past them.

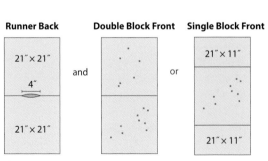

Runner Back

21″ × 21″

4″

21″ × 21″

Figure A

and

Double Block Front

Figure B

or

Single Block Front

21″ × 11″

21″ × 11″

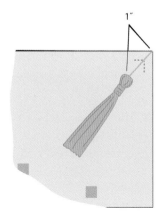

1″

Figure C

6. Place your runner top and assembled backing from Step 2 right sides together. Pin around the edges. See the Creating Sharp Corners note below, and stitch along all 4 sides, pivoting at each corner with the needle down.

FINISHING

1. Reach into the 4″ opening in the runner back created in Step 2 of Assembling and pull the runner right side out. Push out the corners and seams to lay flat. The folded seam allowance corners should pop out neatly, and you can give the tassel a gentle tug to assist.

2. Press the edges and corners flat.

3. Hand-stitch the back closed using a simple whipstitch.

4. Readjusting the stitch length to a regular length on your machine, topstitch around the perimeter of the table runner as closely to the edge as you feel comfortable.

5. Baste the runner by hand (or adjust the stitch length on your machine again and baste by machine) and stitch straight lines about 2″ apart to secure the two layers.

CREATING SHARP CORNERS

Don't clip your corners before turning as you might normally would for a project like this, or you may accidentally clip the tassel tail off. Instead, create sharp corners by folding in the seam allowance and pressing. Fold one seam allowance in right at the stitch line and finger press (Fig. D). Fold the perpendicular seam allowance in and finger press again (Fig E). Repeat at all corners.

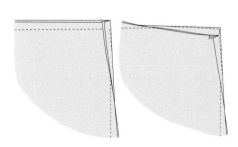

Figure D   Figure E

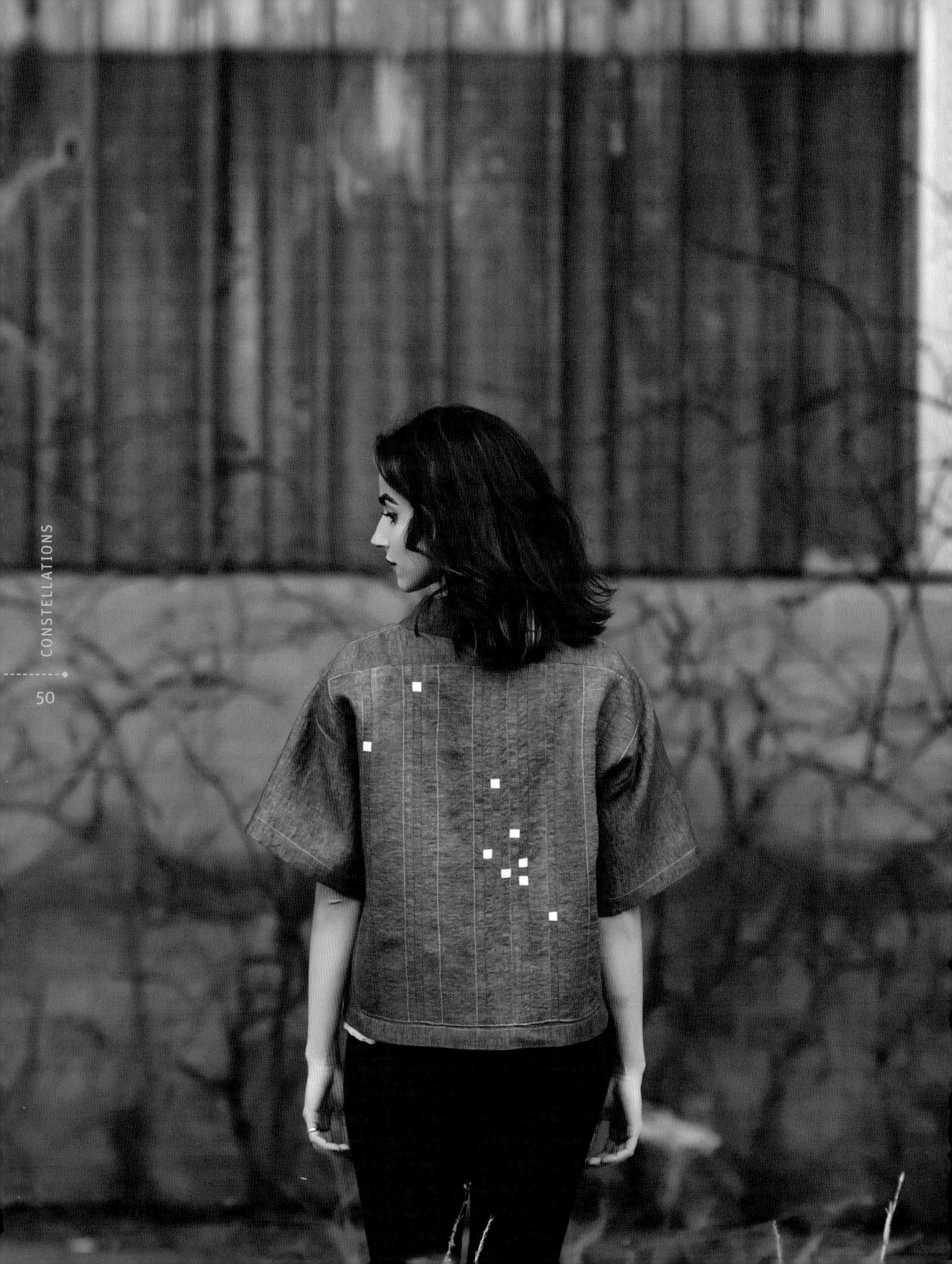

HOSHI JACKET

DESIGNED BY AMBER CORCORAN

This simple, kimono-inspired jacket takes the "quilted jacket" to a new place, showing off your patchwork skills in style. Your star sign in minimal patchwork makes a beautiful statement piece for your wardrobe. Hoshi's unconventional pockets are easily constructed and add visual interest while holding your essentials. Our version is made in a yarn-dyed, lightweight linen in charcoal and natural linen for the stars.

Fabric recommendation: Mid- to light-weight chambray, linen or lightweight denim.

MATERIALS

- ⅝ yard of background fabric for the Constellation Block, plus the jacket yardage listed for the appropriate size in the chart (right).
- ⅛ yard of star fabric
- Coordinating thread to match the background fabric

PATTERN SIZE	A	B	C
SIZE/BUST:	S/M (33 - 36)	L/XL (37 - 42)	XXL (43 - 48)
FINISHED BUST MEASUREMENT	44	50	56
FINISHED HEM MEASUREMENT	46	52	58
YARDAGE FOR JACKET			
44" bolt	2 yards	2 yards	2⅓ yards
60" bolt	1¾ yards	1¾ yards	2 yards

Tools

- rotary cutter and mat
- marking tool
- pattern paper
- fabric shears
- walking foot (optional but helpful)
- seam gauge
- point turner
- hand-sewing needle
- thread

PREPARING THE CONSTELLATION BLOCK

1. Before cutting or assembling the Constellation Block, wash, dry and press all of the fabrics.

2. Cut and assemble your chosen Constellation Block (select from pages 8-33). Center the block and trim to 19" square.

3. Position the trimmed block right side down. With the wrong sides facing, fold all four raw edges over by ½" and press. Using a seam gauge will be helpful here to maintain accuracy.

4. Open up the folded edges from Step 3. Fold one corner in at a 45° angle, at the point where the two creases meet (the creases from Step 3 should also match up). Lightly press to crease at this 45° line. (Fig. A)

5. Open up the fold from Step 4 and position the block wrong side down. Fold two edges of the block corner right sides together, aligning the raw edges and matching the 45° crease to itself.

6. Stitch on the crease from Step 4 being sure to backstitch at the beginning and end. Trim the excess to ⅛" from the stitch line. (Fig. B)

7. Turn the corner right side out. Push out the corner using a point turner to get nice crisp corners and press flat. (Fig. C)

8. Repeat Steps 4-7 for each corner of your block.

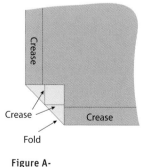

Figure A-

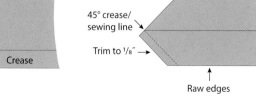

Figure B

Figure C

ASSEMBLING THE JACKET

Use a ½" seam allowance unless directed otherwise, backstitch at the beginning and end of each seam and press after each seam.

1. Using the pattern paper and a pencil, trace all of the pattern pieces for the appropriate size from the pattern pullout. Transfer all of the notches, lines and pattern marks. Cut out the patterns from the pattern paper.

2. Referencing the Cutting Diagrams, fold the background fabric in half lengthwise, wrong sides facing. Position and cut out the pattern pieces from Step 1 using fabric shears.

3. Shorten the stitch length on your machine to 1.8. Using a ⅜" seam allowance, staystitch the collar edge of the Back, and the center front of both Front pieces (Fig. D). Set aside.

Appliquéing the Block

1. Paying attention to the correct orientation, position the prepared block onto the Back piece, both right sides up, matching at the marks. Pin into place.

2. If you have one, install a walking foot onto your machine. Starting at the bottom center of the block, edgestitch around the entire perimeter to secure the block, pivoting with needle down at each corner. Overlap the beginning and end of your stitching by ½".

3. Position the Back on a flat surface and baste the layers together using pins. Stitch vertical straight lines through both layers about 2" apart, just within the edgestitching.

4. Switch back to a regular sewing machine foot and set the assembled Back panel aside.

Assembling and Attaching the Pocket

1. Hem the top of one Pocket piece by turning under the raw edge at ¼" with wrong sides facing, pressing, then turning under again at ½" and pressing again (Fig. E). Edgestitch the hem along the inner fold.

2. To attach the Pocket and hem one jacket Front at the same time, use a French seam. Position the Pocket on top of the Front

Cutting Diagrams

44" wide fabric

60" wide fabric

Figure D

folds ½" wide

Figure E

with both right sides facing up and aligning the bottom raw edges. Pin and sew along the bottom edge using a scant ¼″ seam allowance. Trim the seam allowance to ⅛″. (Fig. F)

3. Open the assembled unit from Step 2 and press the seam allowance towards the Pocket. With the right side of the Pocket facing the wrong side of the Front, encase the raw edges inside the fold (Fig. G). Press the seam flat.

4. Stitch along the folded bottom edge using a ¼" seam allowance. Open the pieces and press the seam allowance towards the Front. Position the Pocket on top of the Front again, so both right sides are facing up. Press the seam flat and baste both sides of the Pocket to the Front using a ¼″ seam allowance. (Fig. H)

5. Using a standard stitch length, topstitch on the marked Pocket stitching line to separate the Pocket into two. Begin stitching from the bottom of the Pocket, and stop ¼″ past the top hem of the Pocket. Backstitch ½″ back to secure your stitching. Before cutting your thread, add additional strength to the Pocket seam by reducing your stitch length, switching to a narrow zig-zag and then stitching back over your backstitch with a narrow satin stitch for ½″ (Fig. I). Set aside.

6. Repeat Steps 1-5 for the remaining Pocket and Front pieces.

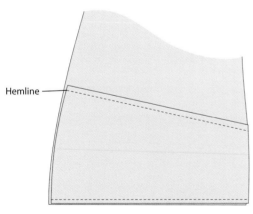

Hemline

Figure F

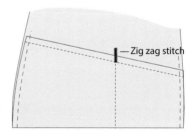

Zig zag stitch

Figure I

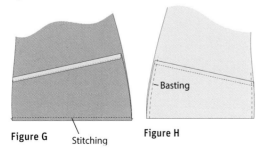

Stitching

Figure G   Stitching

Basting

Figure H

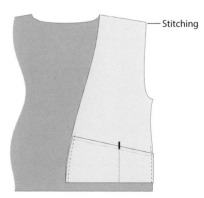

Stitching

Figure J

Seaming the Shoulders

1. Place an assembled Front/Pocket and the Back piece wrong sides together aligning the raw edges at the shoulder. Stitch together at the shoulder and press the seams open. (Fig. J)

2. Trim *only* the Front side of the seam allowance to a scant ¼″. Do not trim the Back seam allowance. (Fig. K)

3. Press the wider seam allowance over the seam towards the Front. Tuck this edge under the trimmed seam allowance to encase the raw edges and press flat towards the Front.

4. Edgestitch along this folded edge to secure the flat felled seam, trapping all raw edges neatly inside. (Fig. L)

5. Repeat for the other shoulder seam with the remaining assembled Front/Pocket piece.

Assembling and Attaching the Collar

1. Stitch the Collar pieces together along one short edge. Press the seam open. This seamline is the center back.

2. Press the assembled Collar from Step 1 in half lengthwise, wrong sides together. Open up the Collar so that you can see the crease.

3. The Collar is attached to the assembled jacket one side at a time. Match and pin the Collar center back with the center back neck of the jacket Back, right sides together. Stitch from the center back across the back neck, over the shoulder seam, and down the center front of the jacket, aligning the raw edges of the Collar and the Front as you sew (Fig. M). The Collar will extend beyond the Front at the bottom. Stop stitching at the bottom of the Front.

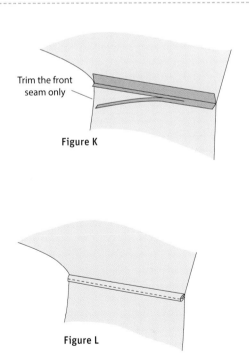

Trim the front seam only

Figure K

Figure L

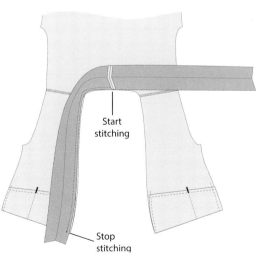

Start stitching

Stop stitching

Figure M

4. Repeat Step 3 for the other side of the jacket, overlapping the start of your stitching by ½" at the center back.

5. Press the seam allowances towards the Collar along the entire length, including the seam allowance extending beyond the hem edge. (Fig. N)

6. Fold the Collar in half along the lengthwise crease. The raw edge will overlap your previous seam by ½". Tuck this raw edge under with the wrong sides facing, at a scant ½", so that the folded edge just covers the seam, and press. (Fig. O)

7. At this point, you may choose to hand stitch the inside of your Collar down for a tidy and professional finish. If you choose to finish by machine, position the jacket with the Front facing up and pin the hemmed Collar to the jacket Front. Be sure to catch the folded edge

on the inside and make sure to pin sufficiently so that the Collar does not shift while you sew it into place. (Fig. P)

8. Before stitching the Collar into place, trim the excess Collar ½" away from the bottom of the Pocket. Tuck the ends of Collar inside, aligning the folded edge with the bottom of the Pocket (Fig. Q). Pin and press in place.

9. Sew into place along the Collar seam, being sure to catch the wrong side of the pressed Collar inside the jacket. Remove the pins just before you get to them and slip-stitch both ends of the Collar closed by hand. (Fig. R)

Attaching the Sleeves

1. Position one Sleeve and the assembled jacket right sides together, aligning the curved raw edges and matching the shoulder

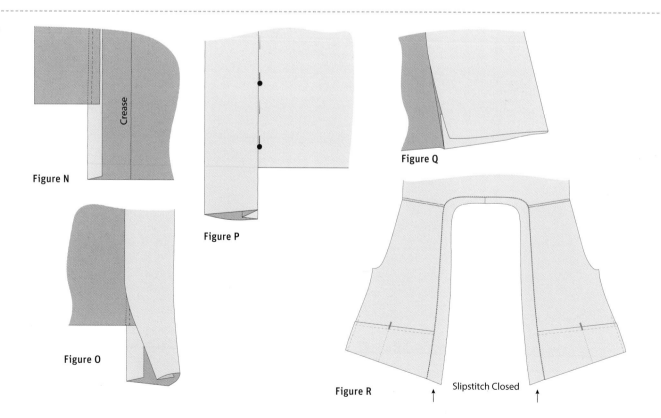

Figure N

Figure O

Figure P

Figure Q

Figure R

Slipstitch Closed

and underarm marks. Pin and stitch through both layers. (Fig. S)

2. Press the seam towards the Sleeve and finish the seam allowance with a zig-zag stitch or using a serger.

3. Repeat Steps 1 and 2 to attach the second Sleeve.

Finishing the Jacket

1. With the wrong sides facing, pin the side seams together. Start at the lower edge of the Sleeve, aligning the raw edges at the underarm seam, and continuing down one side of the jacket towards the bottom edge. The unfinished back will extend 1¼″ beyond the finished front.

2. Sew the side seam. Finish the seam allowance by sewing along the raw edges using a serger or zig-zag stitch (Fig. T). Continuing the seam, finish straight down the excess back seam allowance. Press all seam allowances towards the back.

3. As you did with hemming the Pocket, turn the raw edge of one Sleeve under at ¼″ and press. Turn under again at 1″ and press. Edgestitch along the inner fold to secure the sleeve hem.

4. Repeat Steps 1-4 for the second Sleeve.

5. Following the method from Step 4, hem the jacket Back the same way as the Sleeve, so that the finished length of the Back matches the Front. Slip-stitch the hem closed at the side seam. (Fig. U)

Tada! Now you're ready to dazzle everyone in your new Hoshi Jacket!

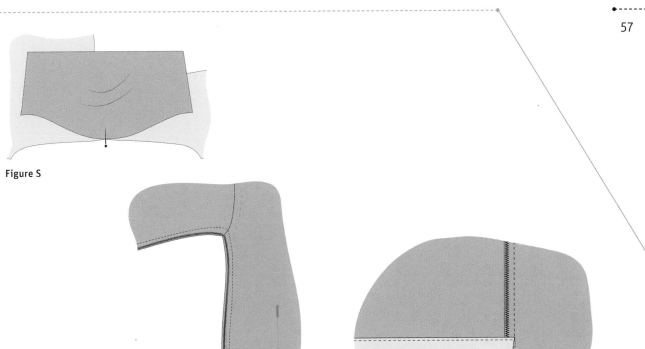

Figure S

Figure T

Figure U

Slipstitch Closed

ASTROLOGICAL
TEA TOWEL

DESIGNED BY AMBER CORCORAN

This sweet tea towel will spruce up any kitchen. It's a great project for fussy cutting. By cutting each star square from a small star print fabric you can give your patchwork a darling finished look. Choose a print with stars that are about ½″ in size. Once you've made your block, try embellishing it before sewing your towel. See page 74 for diagrams of the constellation lines and page 80 for our two favorite embroidery stitches. If you have some trim that you are eager to use, this is the perfect project for it. I used some contrasting mini pom-pom trim from our store. Whether you leave your towel simple or add a lot of embellishments, this project is both practical and beautiful.

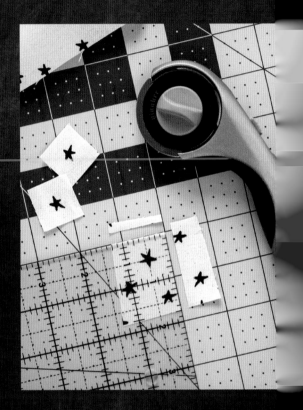

MATERIALS

- 2 yards linen background fabric
- ⅛ yard or mix of scraps for fussy cutting stars
- Embroidery floss (optional)
- ¾ yard mini pom-pom or rickrack trim

CUTTING

For the Constellation Block, cut the background and star fabrics according to the block's specifications (see pages 8–33).

From the remaining background fabric, cut:

(1) 21″ × 31″ rectangle for the towel front

ASSEMBLING

Note: Use a ½" seam allowance when assembling this project.

1. Referencing the patterns in pages 8–33, assemble your chosen Constellation Block and trim to 21" square. If you want to embroider or otherwise fancy-up your block, this is the time to do it (see pages 74–80 for embellishment ideas).

2. With the right sides together, align the 31" towel front rectangle with the top edge of your Constellation Block. Sew together along the 21" edge to complete the towel front. Press the seam to one side.

3. Place the towel back pieces right sides together and sew along the 21" edge, leaving a 3" opening at the center of this seam (Fig. A). Press the seam open.

4. If you are attaching trim, position your assembled towel front piece from Step 2 right side up. Place the trim along the bottom edge of the Constellation Block, with the right side of the trim facing the block (Fig. B). Align the edge of the trim that will be hidden in the seam allowance with the raw edge of the block. Use a basting stitch and a ½" seam allowance to baste the trim in place. Clip off any excess trim from the sides.

Towel Backing

21" × 26"

3"

21" × 26"

Figure A

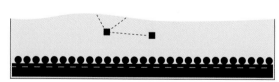

Figure B

5. Position the assembled towel front from Step 2 and the assembled towel back from Step 3 right sides together. Pin to secure and stitch around the entire perimeter of the towel with a ½″ seam allowance.

6. Trim the corners to reduce some of the fabric bulk, being careful not to cut through your stitching. (Fig. C)

7. Reach into the 3″ opening in the towel back and pull the towel right side out. Use a point turner or similar blunt object to help push out the corners, so that they are nice and sharp.

8. Press the edges and corners flat.

9. Hand-stitch the back closed using a simple whipstitch.

10. Topstitch around the perimeter of the towel as close to the edge as you feel comfortable, going slowly and carefully around the trimmed edge (if using).

11. Baste the towel with pins and stitch straight lines along the length of the towel about 2″ apart to secure the two layers.

tip

If you have chosen to add trim to your towel, stitch slowly along the edge where the trim is placed to keep your stitches consistent and to avoid catching any of the decorative details in the seam when you sew the front and back panels together.

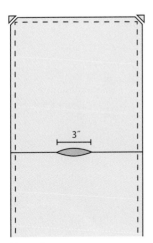

Figure C

CONSTELLATION THROW PILLOW

DESIGNED BY AMBER CORCORAN

This throw pillow celebrates the wonders of the stars with a single Constellation Block. Make one pillow, a pair, or even more, featuring any of the astrological constellations. I especially like how Orion looks, neatly framed within the pillow top. As one of the most recognizable constellations in the night sky, Orion is the perfect choice for dark sky enthusiasts. Orion, the hunter, is easily identified worldwide by the three bright stars on Orion's belt.

MATERIALS

- ⅝ yard background fabric
- ⅛ yard or mix of scraps for stars
- ⅝ yard pillow backing fabric
- 20″ square pillow form
- Embroidery floss (optional)

CUTTING

For the Constellation Block, cut the background and star fabrics according to the block's specifications (see pages 8–33).

From the backing fabric, cut:
  (2) 14″ × 21″ rectangles

ASSEMBLING

Note: Use a ½″ seam allowance when assembling this project.

1. Referencing the Constellation Blocks shown on pages 8–33, assemble your chosen Block and trim to 21″ square.

2. Place a backing rectangle wrong side up, on a flat surface. Fold over a 21″ edge, wrong sides together, by ⅛″ and press. Turn the pressed folded edge over again, this time at ½″ and press again. Stitch this hem down on the inner folded edge. (Fig. A)

3. Repeat Step 2 for the remaining backing rectangle.

4. Position the Constellation Block right side up. Place both pillow backing pieces right side down on top of the block, aligning the raw edges (the panels will overlap in the center). Pin around the edge. (Fig. B)

5. Stitch around the perimeter of the pillow, pivoting at each corner with the needle down. Trim the corners. (Fig. C)

6. Reach into the pillow back and pull the pillow right side out. Push out the corners using a point turner or similar blunt object.

7. Press the edges and corners flat. Tuck your pillow form into the case to finish your pillow.

tip

If you would like to add embroidery embellishments, check out the diagrams on page 74 and embroider the lines using a running stitch (instructions on page 80).

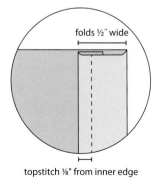

folds ½″ wide

topstitch ⅛″ from inner edge

Figure A

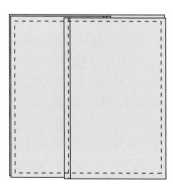

Figure B

Figure C

Finished Size: 20″ square

ZODIAC DIVINATION CLOTH

DESIGNED BY JAIME JENNINGS

This divination cloth is perfect to use for your tarot readings or as a ritual altar cloth. This simple cloth is constructed with two Constellation Blocks that are inverse colors—one with light background and one with dark background. Use the cloth with either side up depending on whether a dark moon or a full moon, or upon your mood-of-the-moment or future plans.

MATERIALS

A silky, lightweight fabric is best for this project to create an ethereal cloth. The sample is made using a viscose batiste, a very lightweight rayon fabric, for the background and the stars. Other options that would make a beautiful choice are rayon, silk blends, or cotton cupro.

- ⅝ yard light background fabric
- ⅝ yard dark background fabric
- ⅛ yard light star fabric
- ⅛ yard dark star fabric

tip

When sewing with slippery fabrics, a spray stabilizer can really help. Spray it onto the fabric before cutting your pieces, and your sewing will go much easier. Also helpful are silk pins and a microtex machine needle.

ASSEMBLING

Note: Use a ½″ seam allowance when assembling this project.

1. Choose two Constellation Blocks — one will use a dark background and light stars and the other will use a light background and dark stars. Referencing pages 8–33 and using appropriate fabrics, assemble your chosen blocks and trim each to 21″ square.

2. Position the assembled Constellation Blocks right sides together. Beginning in the middle of one raw edge, stitch around all 4 sides, pivoting at each corner with the needle down. Stop sewing 3″ from where you began.

3. Trim the corners being careful not to cut your stitching. (Fig. A)

4. Turn the assembled unit from Step 2 right side out and push out the corners using a point turner or similar blunt object. Carefully press using a pressing cloth.

5. Turn in the opening's raw edges ½″, wrong sides facing, and press using a pressing cloth.

6. Topstitch around the entire outer edge of the divination cloth, closing the opening as you sew.

tip

I used a different color top and bobbin thread that matched the light and dark fabrics on each side.

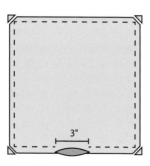

Figure A

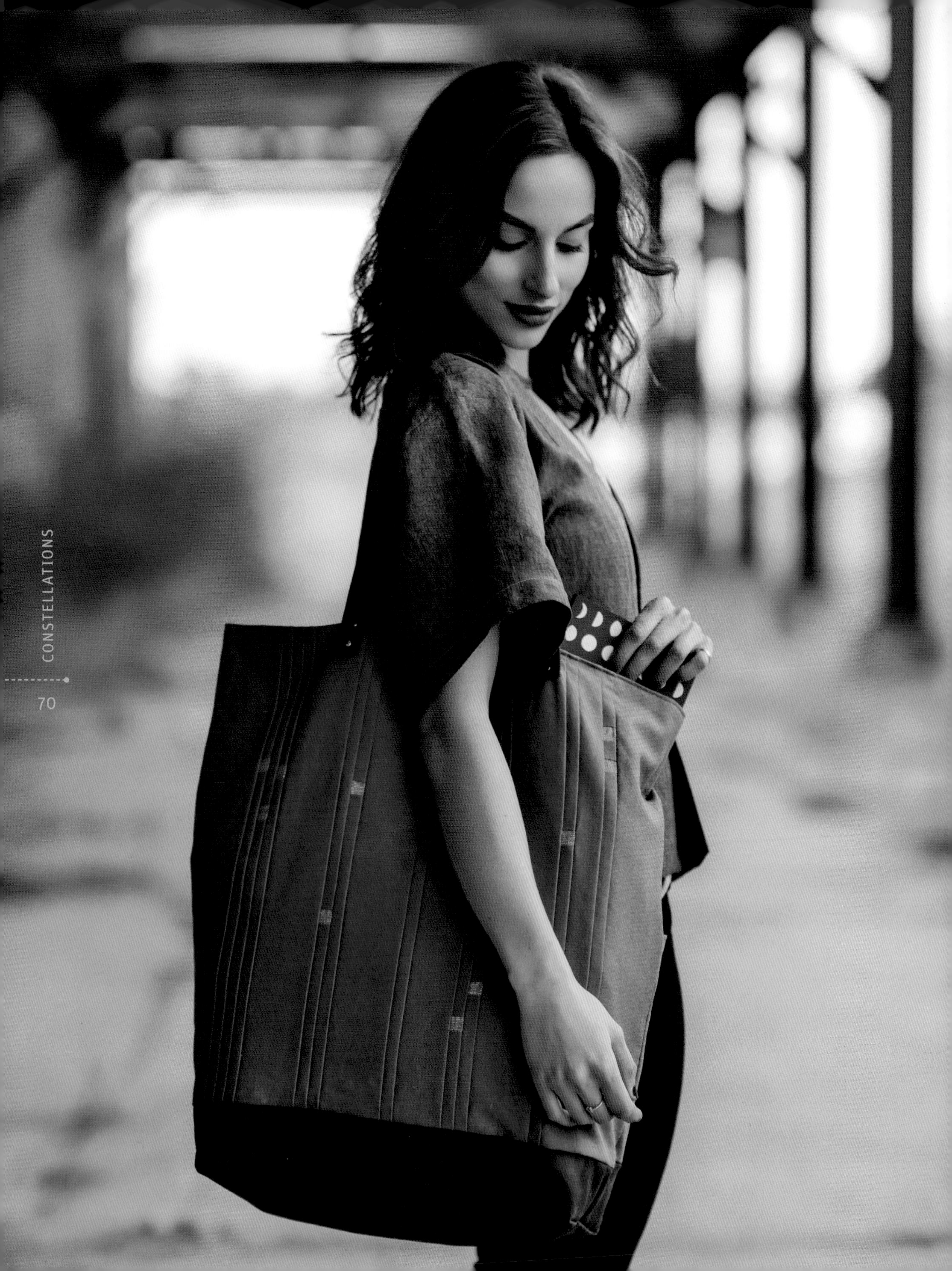

STAR SIGN TOTE

DESIGNED BY JAIME JENNINGS

This sophisticated tote combines a pieced Constellation Block with a waxed canvas bottom and leather handles for a sturdy and stylish oversize bag. Using durable, medium to heavy weight fabrics will give this large bag structure and stability. We used a linen/cotton canvas, but home dec fabric would work great as well. Outside pockets make it easy to find your keys and phone. A lined hard plastic insert in the bottom of the bag helps this tote retain its shape, and the bag is finished with a snap closure.

MATERIALS

- 1½ yards mid-heavy weight background fabric for the Block, Back panel and Pockets
- ⅛ yard or mix of scraps for the Stars
- ¾ yard waxed canvas for the Base
- 1 yard mid-heavy weight fabric for the Lining
- 8 double-cap small rivets if your handle set does not come with them
- (1) 6″ × 13″ rectangle extra-heavy template plastic
- (2) 1″ × 24″ leather handles, or pre-made leather handles of your choice
- 1″ magnetic snap closure
- Water-soluble pen

CUTTING

For the Constellation Block, cut the background and star fabrics according to the block's specifications (see pages 8–33).

From the remaining background fabric, cut:
  (1) 18″ × 21″ rectangle for the Exterior
  (2) 9″ × 21″ rectangles for the Pockets

From the Lining fabric, cut:
  (2) 21″ × 23½″ rectangles for the Lining
  (2) 7″ × 14″ rectangles to cover the template plastic

From the waxed canvas, cut:
  (1) 12″ × 21″ rectangle for the Base

ASSEMBLING

Note: Use a ½″ seam allowance throughout.

Referencing pages 8–33 for ideas and using appropriate fabrics, assemble a Constellation Block. Trim the block to 21″ wide × 18″ tall.

The Pocket

1. Position the (2) 9″ × 21″ background rectangles right sides together and sew along one long edge. Press the seam open.

2. Position the wrong sides together. Press the folded seam flat and topstitch along the long folded edge.

3. With the folded edge at the top, use a water-soluble marker and a ruler to mark lines perpendicular to your topstitching from Step 2 at 7″ and 13″ away from the left raw edge but do not sew along them yet. (Fig. A)

4. Position the Pocket on the right side of the 18″ × 21″ Back, aligning the raw edges of the bottom and sides. Using the longest stitch, machine baste the sides using a ¼″ seam allowance here.

5. Switch your machine back to a normal stitch setting. Starting at the bottom of the Pocket, sew through all layers along the marked lines from Step 3, being sure to backstitch at the top of the Pocket.

The Exterior

1. With the right sides together, align a long edge of the waxed canvas with the bottom of the Pocket on the Back. Sew along this edge, then press the seam towards the waxed canvas.

2. With right sides together, align the bottom edge of the Constellation Block with the opposide side of the waxed canvas. Sew and press the seam towards the waxed canvas. (Fig. B)

3. Fold the assembled unit in half with right sides together, aligning the waxed canvas seams from Step 2 (Fig. C). Pin or clip along the raw edges of the long sides.

4. Ensuring that the top edges are aligned, stitch along the sides of the pinned bag, beginning by backstitching at the top and sewing down the length towards the waxed canvas. Press the seams open.

5. Box the corners so the bag will sit flat. With the bag still wrong side out, pinch one of the sewn corners and position the bag so the side and bottom seams meet, forming a point. Press. Measure 3″ down from the point and mark a horizontal line with a water-soluble pen. Sew along the marked line. Using a ruler, cut away the excess fabric, leaving ½″ seam allowance (Fig. D). Repeat on the other corner.

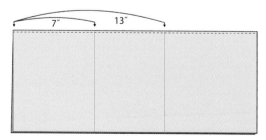

Figure A

Figure B

tip

When pressing waxed canvas be sure to use a pressing cloth or scrap fabric between your iron and the waxed canvas, and set your iron to a medium heat. You can also choose to finger press the seams. Test with scraps for the best result.

The Lining

1. Position the (2) 21″ × 23½″ lining rectangles right sides together and stitch along both long sides. Press the seams open.

2. Stitch along one of the short edges, leaving a 6″ opening for turning.

3. Box the corners of the lining as you did in Step 5 of the Exterior.

The Body of the Bag

1. With a water-soluble pen, mark a dot on each lining piece 2″ away from the top edge and centered across the width. Using these dots for placement and, following the manufacturer's instructions, attach the magnetic snap closure to the right sides of the Lining. (Fig.E)

2. Turn right side out and place the Lining inside of the Exterior, right sides facing. Align the raw edges at the top and pin to secure.

3. Sew around the entire perimeter of the top. Turn the bag right side out through the 6″ gap in the bottom of the Lining.

4. Press the top of the bag and topstitch around ⅛″ from the edge.

5. Close the opening in the Lining by sewing very close to the edge with your machine or hand-stitching with a slipstitch.

The Handles

1. Using a water-soluble pen and a ruler, measure from one edge of the bag 1¼″ from the top raw edge and mark at both 4″ and 5″. Place one end of a leather handle in between these marks (Fig. F). Follow the manufacturer's instructions to attach the handle with two rivets.

2. Repeat on the same side of the bag opening to attach the other end of the handle. Before installing the rivets, make sure the handle is not twisted.

3. Repeat Steps 1-2 to attach the second handle to the opposite side of the bag.

Finishing

1. Position the (2) 7″ × 14″ plastic lining rectangles right sides together. Sew along both long sides and one short side, pivoting at each corner with the needle down. Trim the corners, being careful not to cut through your stitching.

2. Turn the assembled unit right side out and slip the template plastic inside.

3. Fold the unsewn edge in snugly and slipstitch or topstitch closed. Place the covered plastic piece in the bottom of your bag to add structure to the base.

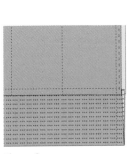

Figure C

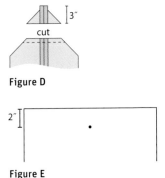

cut

Figure D

2″

Figure E

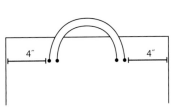

4″   4″

Figure F

PART 3

DIAGRAMS + TECHNIQUES

Use these lines to connect your stars in any of the projects. You can embroider these lines on your block or use them as a guide for quilting. Use a water-soluble marking tool and a ruler to mark the constellation lines on your block. For embroidery embellishment, once you complete a block and before proceeding with your project, add embroidery embellishments (see embroidering techniques on page 80. If you are using the lines as a guide for your quilting, mark lines once you are ready to quilt.

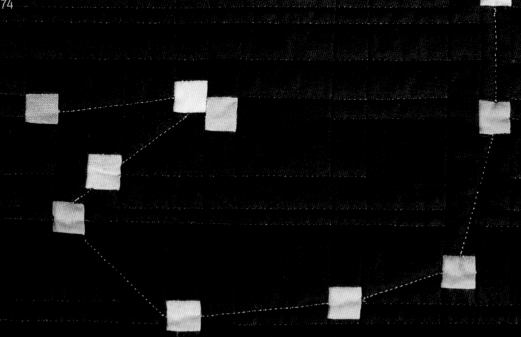

DIAGRAMS OF CONSTELLATION LINES
FOR EMBROIDERY OR QUILTING

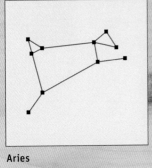

Aries

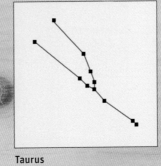

Taurus

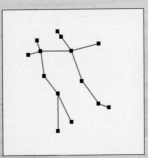

Gemini

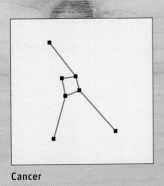

Cancer

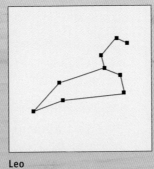

Leo

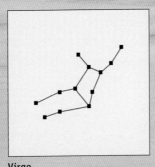

Virgo

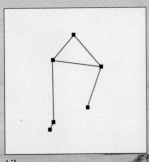

Libra

Scorpio

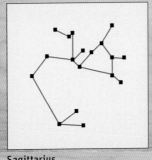

Sagittarius

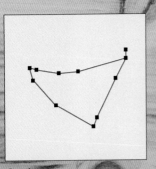

Capricorn

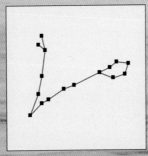

Aquarius

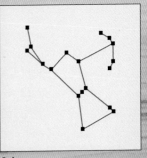

Pieces

Orion

STAR STITCH QUILT TYING TECHNIQUE

Hand tying is a quick way to secure the layers of a quilt and gives a quilt a soft finish. We find this technique especially endearing and nostalgic. This method can be used to tie a quilt of any size. If you plan to bind the layers of your quilt together, you will baste and tie the quilt before attaching your binding or after turning if using an envelope turning method.

MATERIALS

- Quilt sandwich, prior to basting or binding
- Crewel wool (or other floss)
- Long, sharp needle with a large enough eye for your chosen floss
- Safety pins
- Marking tool

Instructions

1. Mark all of your desired tie placements on the quilt top using a water-soluble pen or tailor's chalk. Depending on the density of the batting you use, the ties should be between 4″ and 6″ apart. Baste the quilt with safety pins to keep the layers from shifting.

2. Thread the needle with floss about a yard long (we used a single strand of crewel wool, but you could also use 6-stranded floss). To start the first tie, with the quilt front on top, insert your needle about 3″ from your first mark, going only through the top layer of fabric. Catching the batting is okay, but use your hand behind the quilt to feel your needle and make sure it doesn't catch the back.

3. Bring the needle back out to the front side of the quilt at your mark (Figs. A and B). Pull the floss gently until the tail is drawn just inside the fabric, leaving a 3″ tail between the batting and the quilt top.

4. Anchor the tail of the floss within the layers by holding with your non-sewing hand. Insert the needle back down about ⅜″ away from your last stitch, going straight through all of the layers. Pull the floss through to the back of quilt (Fig. C), being careful for the first few stitches to keep your tail anchored within the quilt.

5. Bring the needle back up through all the layers, placing it ¼″ away from and centered right next to the stitch from Steps 3 and 4. Pull your thread all the way through to the front but not pulling too tightly so as to pucker the quilt.

6. Cross over the previous stitch to make a "+" and insert your needle through the top layer only. Staying just beneath the quilt top, bring the needle back out to the front side at your next mark. (Figs. D and E)

7. Draw the floss gently through the quilt until the remaining floss is pulled through the top, but make sure it is not taut or tugging the stitches together. (Fig. F)

8. Your first "star stitch tie" is complete. There is a "+" on the front of quilt and a "–" on the back. (Fig. G)

9. Repeat Steps 4–7 (Fig. H) until you have stitched all your quilt ties.

10. To secure the last stitch, insert the needle just through the top layer and come out about 3″ away from your last stitch. Clip the floss right next to the fabric and give the fabric a little tug so that the end of the 3″ tail goes inside the quilt.

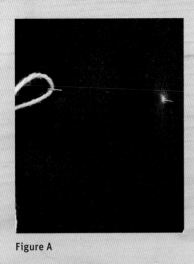

Figure A

Figure B

Figure C

Figure D

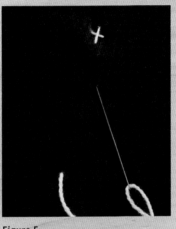

Figure E

Figure F

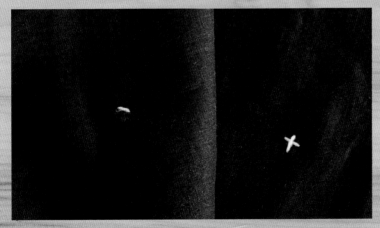

Figure G

Figure H

MAKING TASSELS

Attach these decorative tassels to any of your projects. They can be seen on the Celestial Table Runner project on page 46. These tassel instructions make a 2½" long tassel. To make tassels of different sizes, change the size of your cardboard piece to the length you would like to make. Use more wraps or a chunkier yarn to make a heftier tassel.

page 46

MATERIALS

- Cotton embroidery floss (1 skein makes two 2½" tassels)
- Cardboard (or heavy card stock)
- Embroidery needle
- Scissors

Instructions

1. Cut a piece of cardboard 2½" square.

2. Cut a 10" length of embroidery floss. Fold the thread in half and lay it across the top of the square card. (Fig. A)

3. With the cut end positioned at the bottom of the card, wrap a length of embroidery floss 20 times around the card. Leave a 12" tail and cut off the excess thread. (Fig. B)

4. The original 10" length is now between the cardboard and the wraps with a loop on one side and two tails on the other. Bring the two tails through the loop, and pull on them to cinch the loop around the wraps at the top of the card. (Fig. C)

5. Slide the wraps off the card and thread the 12" tail onto a needle.

6. Draw the needle through the center of the wraps near the top of the tassel. (Fig. D)

7. Remove the needle and wrap the tail around the tassel somewhat tightly, starting near the top and wrapping slowly downward for about ½". (Fig. E)

8. Thread the tail onto the needle again and draw the tail up through the inside of these wraps. (Fig. F)

9. Weave back down, skipping over a few wraps to secure the tail from being pulled back through. (Fig. G)

10. Cut the bottom loops of the tassel and trim any remaining tail. (Fig. H)

11. Take the two strands at the top of the tassel and make a square knot cord (Fig. I). Tie a sequence of knots, alternating them until your cord is about 1" long (Fig. J):

> Right thread over left, around the back and through.

> Left thread over right, around the back and through.

Your tassel is complete!

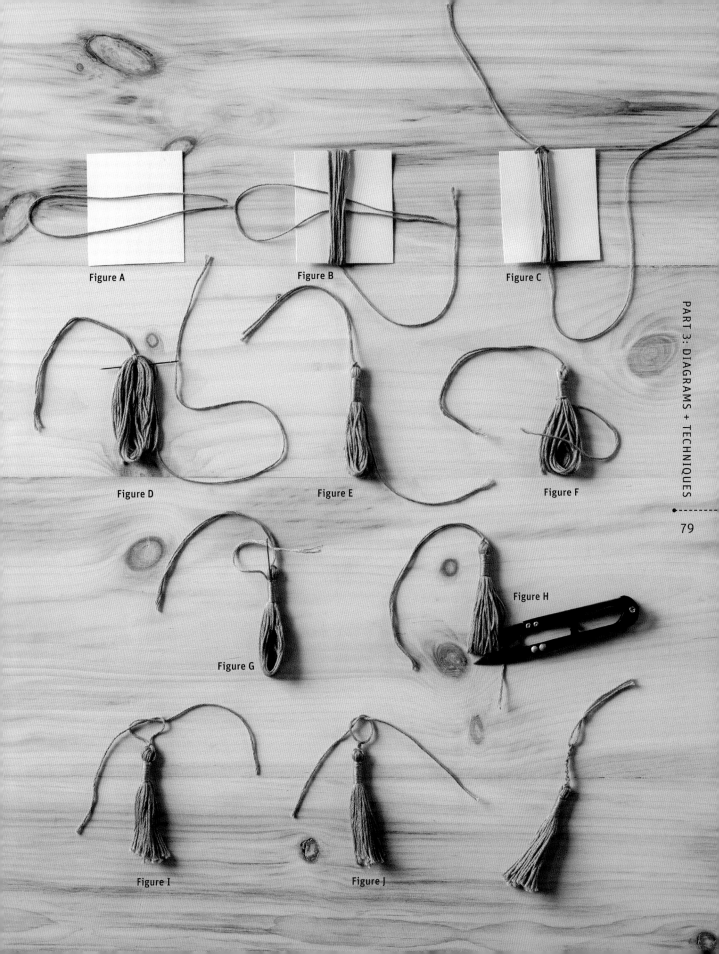

Figure A

Figure B

Figure C

Figure D

Figure E

Figure F

Figure G

Figure H

Figure I

Figure J

EMBROIDERING WITH SIMPLE STITCHES

Consider adding either of these simple embroidery methods for linework. The backstitch was used for the lettering on the Baby Quilt on page 42. We used the running stitch for the constellation in the Tea Towel project on page 58.

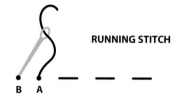

Backstitch

The backstitch creates a solid line and can be used to embroider names, dates, or lines. It is called a backstitch because you start by coming up where your stitch ends and then stitch "back" to the beginning of the stitch. This allows the stitches to be right next to each other, creating a solid line.

BACKSTITCH

A

B A

1. Tie a knot at the end of your floss. Start your first stitch by coming up from the back of the fabric about a stitch length beyond where you want your line to begin (A).

2. Finish the stitch by going back to the beginning of your line (B).

3. From the back of your fabric, come up a stitch length beyond the end of your previous stitch.

4. Repeat Steps 2 and 3 until you have completed your line.

5. Secure your thread on the back of the fabric.

Running Stitch

The running stitch creates a broken, or dotted, line. It is quick and simple to do, but make sure you don't pull the thread too tightly as you sew or your fabric may pucker. It is important to pay attention to the spacing between each stitch. Try to keep all of your stitches a consistent length.

RUNNING STITCH

B A

1. Tie a knot at the end of your floss. Start your first stitch by coming up from the back of the fabric right where you want your line to begin (A).

2. Finish the stitch by going back in one stitch length away (B).

3. From the back of your fabric, come up half a stitch length beyond the end of your previous stitch.

4. Repeat Steps 2 and 3 until you have completed your line.

5. Secure your thread on the back of the fabric.